i lian
sence

ATUL KOCHHAR

PHOTOGRAPHS BY DAVID LOFTUS

indian
essence

THE FRESH TASTES OF INDIA'S NEW CUISINE

QUADRILLE

To my beautiful baby daughter Amisha

Publishing director Anne Furniss
Art director Helen Lewis
Project editor Janet Illsley
Senior designer Jim Smith
Photographer David Loftus
Food stylist Atul Kochhar
Props stylist Jane Campsie
Production Beverley Richardson

First published in 2004 by
Quadrille Publishing Limited
Alhambra House
27-31 Charing Cross Road
London WC2H OLS

This paperback edition first published in 2005
10 9 8 7 6 5 4 3 2

ISBN 1 84400 151 2
Printed and bound in China

NOTES
- All recipes serve 4 as part of an Indian meal featuring a selection of dishes, unless otherwise indicated.
- Ingredients highlighted with an asterisk are explained in the glossary on pages 156–7.
- All spoon measures are level unless otherwise stated: 1 tsp = 5ml spoon; 1 tbsp = 15 ml spoon.
- Use fresh herbs unless dried herbs are suggested.
- Use sea salt and freshly ground black pepper unless otherwise stated.
- All vegetables and fruit should be washed and peeled as normal.
- Ovens and grills must be preheated to the setting specified in the recipe.

I would like to thank the Almond Board
of California very much for all their help
and support during this exciting project.

CONTENTS

INTRODUCTION

Indian food is as diverse as its culture, geography and climate. It is vibrant, colourful, enticing, easy to prepare and wonderfully satisfying. The essence of good Indian cooking revolves around the appropriate use of aromatic spices. Spicing is not a difficult concept. In the same way that salt and pepper are used in the West, the skill lies in using spices to enhance rather than overwhelm the intrinsic flavour of a particular dish.

From a young age, an Indian child is exposed to an extraordinary array of flavour combinations, probably more so than in any other civilisation. Indian cuisine is based on a variety of flavour sensations, which encompasses hot and sour, hot and nutty, sweet and hot, bitter and hot, bitter and sour, to name but a few. In seasoning, it ranges from the freshness and sweetness of aromatic curry leaves to the dark pungency of the resin, asafoetida. Indian genius lies not only in combining seasonings, but also in drawing out several flavours from a single spice – by roasting, grinding or frying – to create a vast spectrum of flavours.

Indians are adventurous and there is nothing that cannot be spiced up in an Indian kitchen, but it is important to understand the distinction between spice and heat. In India, heat is generally applied with chillies and selectively, whereas spicing is all about flavouring. In the south, chilli heat is valued for its ultimate cooling effect on the body, by inducing perspiration. In the north, dishes are not overly hot – it's all about bringing out the best of the spices. Though, of course, there are always pickles and chutneys to impart fiery heat if required.

Indian ingredients and spices are relatively easy to source these days. Most supermarkets now stock a good range of spices and ethnic ingredients, and Asian food stores – offering fresh vegetables and fruits, as well as specialist dried goods – are everywhere. If you do not have an Asian food store or well-stocked supermarket nearby, surf the net for a mail order alternative – you will find several specialist Indian food suppliers. You may also be able to buy ingredients in delicatessens and other food stores. Many Egyptian, Iranian and Moroccan ingredients, for example, are similar to Indian items.

Religious and regional influences

Religion is said to be the most important aspect of Indian life and food its most precious resource. The majority of Indians are vegetarian due to their belief in Hinduism, Jainism or Buddhism. Certain foods are deemed pure or sacred and feature prominently in temple rituals. Food also plays an important role in the numerous festivals and ceremonies across the sub-continent. Often a festival is associated with a particular food – sweet semolina pancakes, for example, are synonymous with *holi*, the festival of colour.

Although a number of religions exist in India, the two cultures that have influenced Indian cooking and food habits more than any other are the Hindu and Muslim traditions. Each new wave of settlers brought with them their own culinary practices. However, over time, they adopted specialities and cooking techniques from the Indian cuisine and merged them with their own to perfection. The Portuguese, Persians and British made important contributions to the Indian culinary scene. For example, it was the British who started the commercial cultivation of tea in India.

The Hindu vegetarian custom is widespread in India, although many Hindus now eat meat. The Muslim tradition is most evident in the cooking of meats. *Mughlai* food, *kababs*, rich *kormas* (curries) and *nargisi koftas* (meat balls), *biryani*, *rogan josh,* and preparations from the clay oven or *tandoor*, like *tandoori rotis* and *tandoori* chicken, are contributions from the Muslim settlers in India.

As India is such a vast country, food customs vary from region to region. The north is the culinary heart of India, with Delhi at the hub, and this was the first regional cuisine to set foot outside India. The food is rich and colourful, and the spicing is generally very aromatic. Wheat is the staple food and *roti* (bread) is served at every meal. A typical north Indian meal would consist of *chapattis* (unleavened bread baked on a griddle) or *parathas* (unleavened bread fried on a griddle), rice and an assortment of dishes like dals, fried vegetables, curries, paneer, chutney and pickles. Most north Indian desserts are similar in taste as they are derived from a milk pudding or rice base and are usually soaked in syrup. *Kheer,* a form of rice pudding, and *kulfi*, a nutty ice cream are typical northern desserts.

South India comprises Andhra Pradesh, Tamil Nadu, Karnataka and Kerala. The food is generally light, non-greasy and fragrant with curry leaves, coconut and spices. Indeed, this is the main region for the production of spices. Rice is the staple food and forms the basis of every meal. It is usually served with *rasam* (a thin soup), *sambhar* (lentil preparation), dry and curried vegetables, and a curd preparation called *pachadi*. Coconut is an important ingredient in south Indian food. *Dosas* (rice pancakes) and *idli* (steamed rice cakes) are now popular throughout the country. Keralan specialities include *appams* (rice pancakes) and thick aromatic stews.

The food in the western states – Maharashtra, Gujarat, Rajasthan, Goa and Madhya Pradesh – varies significantly from state to state. Rajasthan, for example, is known for its robust meat and poultry dishes, while Gujarat is home to superb, fresh-tasting and light vegetarian dishes. East India includes some of the poorest states in India, which is reflected in eating habits, but it makes some interesting culinary contributions, notably with its colourful street foods. The cuisine of Bengal is the most influential and interesting, with a combination of Hindu and Muslim foods.

Planning an Indian menu

In Indian homes, menus are planned around a core recipe. For the majority of Indians who are vegetarian, this will be a lentil or other pulse. Then two, three or four vegetable dishes will be chosen to serve with it. These provide contrast in texture, flavour and colour. Rice or bread (or both) will be served alongside, and a dessert rounds off most meals. For non-vegetarians, there may be two core recipes – featuring seafood, poultry, game or meat – plus two or three vegetables, a lentil dish, rice and/or bread, with a dessert to follow.

Indians are enthusiastic hosts, and entertaining menus are often quite ambitious – almost mini banquets. It is not unusual to serve two or three appetisers, two or three core recipes, perhaps four vegetables, rice, one or two types of bread and a couple of desserts. Of course, menus differ from region to region. Among non-vegetarians, north Indians are big meat and poultry eaters; west Indians favour lamb, duck and fish; east Indians like fish, lamb and poultry; while in the south you find fish, game, meat and poultry. Of course, vegetarian dishes are an essential part of any meal, so two or three vegetables are chosen, usually a mixture of root, stem and leafy vegetables for variety.

Although Indians generally prefer to prepare their own regional food, they are adventurous and 'pan-Indian' menus featuring dishes from all over the sub-continent are increasingly common. So, when you are choosing dishes for a meal, don't hesitate to mix and match recipes from different regions. For ideas on composing menus, see my suggestions on pages 154–5. There are no hard and fast rules, so feel free to alter these as you please, aiming to offer a rich variety of flavours, colours and textures – to convey the essence of Indian food.

In India, eating out is a serious business and that is why café and street food is so huge. When they are out and about, people like to grab something to eat while talking, shopping, browsing or conducting business. Most of the foods eaten are comparable to western snacks or starters — and Indians will return home for a proper meal after snacking. In this chapter, I have included a melange of street food, café food, railway platform food, beach food and some traditional regional home cooking. As you would expect, most of the recipes are easy and quick to prepare.

JHAL MURI

Seasoned puff rice BIHAR, EAST INDIA

This was once my favourite food and it still brings back memories of my childhood in east India. *Jhal muri* is eaten as a snack, salad or an appetiser. It is also one of the colourful street foods of eastern India – typically eaten with *channa bhaja* (pressed crisp fried spicy gram) or *channa choor* (chickpea snack). It is quite close to the *bhel puri* and *sev puri* of western India, but it has an eastern flavour profile. *Jhal muri* can include a wide variety of interesting ingredients, but I have kept the combination relatively simple here.

First make the dressing. Put the mustard oil, lime juice, red chilli powder, toasted cumin and mango powder into a small bowl and whisk together until evenly blended. Stir in the tamarind chutney if using, and season with salt to taste. Set aside.

Put the puffed rice into a large bowl, add the sev and toss to mix. Add the chopped onion, potato, tomato, cucumber and green chilli. Mix well, then add the shredded coriander, sprouted beans and peanuts. Mix all the ingredients together, then add the dressing and toss to mix. Pile the salad into a bowl to serve.

Note: Sev is a ready-made Indian snack, best described as crispy deep-fried chickpea flour noodles flavoured with various spices – red chilli powder, fenugreek leaf powder, salt etc. Puffed rice is known by other names, including *muri* in the east and *phuliyan* in the north. Both puffed rice and sev are available from Asian grocers and some supermarkets.

Variation: Use freshly cooked or canned chickpeas instead of the mixed sprouted beans.

250g puffed rice

50g sev (vermicelli-like crisp savoury noodle snack)

½ red onion, finely chopped

½ boiled potato, diced

½ tomato, finely chopped

50g cucumber, finely chopped

1 green chilli, finely chopped

1 tbsp shredded coriander leaves

50g mixed sprouted beans

30g peanuts, roasted or fried and salted (with skins)

DRESSING:

4 tsp mustard oil

2 tsp lime juice

¼ tsp red chilli powder

¼ tsp toasted cumin seeds, crushed

¼ tsp mango powder*

1 tbsp sweet tamarind chutney (page 138, optional)

½ tsp salt, or to taste

PAPARIS RECHEADOS

Stuffed poppadoms   GOA, WEST INDIA

Papads are made from different lentils – the ones made from urad dal are ideal for this recipe. I have filled them with spicy gingery prawns, but you can use a different stuffing, such as spiced mashed potato. Serve with a salad and a spicy chutney – mango and passion fruit chutney (page 140) goes brilliantly and passion fruit are native to Goa.

To make the stuffing, heat the oil in a frying pan, add the onion, garlic, ginger and black pepper, and sauté until the onion is softened and translucent. Add the ground coriander, turmeric and prawns, sauté for 3–4 minutes, then add the potatoes, lemon juice and salt. Sprinkle with the chopped coriander and cinnamon, mix well and set aside to cool.

Meanwhile, soak the papads in warm water for 5–10 minutes to soften, then drain. Mix the flour with a little water to form a paste. Spoon the prawn mixture on to one side of the papads, then roll up, folding in the sides, and seal the edges with flour paste.

Heat the oil for deep-frying in a suitable pan to 160°C. Deep-fry the stuffed papads, a few at a time, for 2–3 minutes until crisp and golden. Drain on kitchen paper and serve hot, with a chutney.

8 plain or spicy papads (uncooked poppadoms)
1 tbsp strong plain flour
vegetable oil, to deep-fry

STUFFING:
1 tbsp vegetable oil
1 large onion, finely chopped
1 tsp finely chopped garlic
1 tbsp finely chopped root ginger
1 tsp freshly ground black pepper
1/4 tsp ground coriander
1/2 tsp ground turmeric
200g cleaned raw prawns, roughly chopped
100g boiled potatoes, roughly chopped
1 tbsp lemon juice
1/2 tsp salt, or to taste
2 tbsp chopped coriander leaves
ground cinnamon, to sprinkle

TARKARI NI BHAJIA

Parsi vegetable fritters   WEST INDIA

I am a true fan of this *bhaji*. The combination of ingredients and spices – and the unusual method – brings out the flavours to the full. Serve hot, with sweet tamarind chutney (page 138).

For the batter, put the tamarind pulp in a bowl with 4 tbsp warm water and leave to soak for 20 minutes, then strain through a fine sieve.

Par-boil the potatoes in salted water for 5–7 minutes, then drain and grate when cool enough to handle. Heat the oil for deep-frying in a suitable pan and deep-fry the onions until lightly caramelised. Remove and drain on kitchen paper; set aside. (Keep the oil to cook the fritters.)

Put the green chillies, coriander leaves, garlic, dried chilli and 1/2 tsp salt in a blender or mini-processor and whiz to a rough paste; set aside.

For the batter, mix the dry ingredients together in a bowl, then add the tamarind juice and 100ml water and mix until smooth.

Mash the bananas in a bowl, then add the potatoes and onion and mix well. Mix in the spicy paste, followed by the batter to make a stiff paste.

Heat the oil for deep-frying to 190°C. With a wet spoon, drop in spoonfuls of mixture and deep-fry in batches for 3–5 minutes until golden. Serve hot.

2 medium potatoes, peeled and quartered
salt
vegetable oil, to deep-fry
2 medium onions, finely sliced
2 green chillies, stems removed
1 tbsp coriander leaves
4 garlic cloves, peeled
1 dried red chilli
2 ripe bananas, peeled

BATTER:
1 tbsp tamarind pulp*
150g gram flour*
1/2 tsp salt
1/2 tsp bicarbonate of soda
1/2 tsp ground turmeric

MOMOS

Indian dim sum ARUNACHAL PRADESH, EAST INDIA

Indian dim sum owe their origin to Tibetan influence on tribal Indian food in Arunachal Pradesh. This north-eastern state is predominantly Buddhist and the sixth Dalai Lama was born here. Momos may have either a vegetarian or non-vegetarian stuffing and are often eaten with a grilled tomato chutney and/or sweet tamarind chutney.

Sift the flour and salt into a bowl, make a well and add 100ml water. Mix to a smooth, firm dough, then knead in the oil. Wrap in cling film and leave to rest for 1 hour. Meanwhile, mix the stuffing ingredients together in a bowl.

Divide the dough into 10 portions and shape into small balls. With a rolling pin, flatten out each ball to a disc and place 1 tsp of stuffing in the centre. Brush the edges of the dough together with water, gather up over the filling and pinch together to seal and form parcels.

Put the dumplings in a steamer over a pan of boiling stock or water with the bay leaf and ginger added. Cover and steam for 10–12 minutes, until cooked through. Serve hot, with chutneys.

200g strong plain flour
1 tsp salt
1½ tbsp vegetable oil
stock, flavoured with bay leaf and ginger, to steam

STUFFING:
100g fine, lean lamb, pork or chicken mince
½ tsp each red chilli powder and ground coriander
10 basil leaves, chopped
½ tsp salt
½ onion, finely chopped
1 green chilli, finely chopped

TO SERVE:
grilled tomato chutney (page 139)
sweet tamarind chutney (page 138)

LITTEE

Spicy stuffed baked dough balls BIHAR, EAST INDIA

A speciality of Bihar, *littee* are similar to the *batti* of Rajasthan and *bafla* of Madhya Pradesh; it is the stuffing that varies. *Littee* use spicy black gram flour, *batti* use spicy green peas, while *bafla* are filled with spicy potato or cornmeal flour. Traditionally, these dough balls are baked on wood or charcoal ashes. They are typically eaten with a potato and cauliflower curry (as illustrated on page 109), or dal.

Sift the flour and salt into a bowl, make a well and add the ginger-garlic paste, green chilli paste and 150–200ml water. Mix well and knead in the ghee to make a smooth, firm dough. Wrap in cling film and leave to rest for 1 hour. Preheat the oven to 190°C (170°C fan oven) mark 5.

Meanwhile, mix all the stuffing ingredients together in a bowl with 2 tbsp water to form a rough crumbly mixture, then set aside.

Divide the dough into 12 balls, 5cm in diameter. Flatten each one just enough to form a hollow for the stuffing. Put in a heaped teaspoonful of stuffing, bring the dough over to enclose and roll again to a ball shape.

Place the dough balls on a greased baking tray and bake for 10 minutes. Turn and bake for a further 10 minutes until the littee are golden brown; a few cracks should appear on the surface. Dip into (or brush with) melted ghee and serve hot, with the cauliflower and potato curry.

500g strong plain flour
1 tsp salt
2 tsp ginger-garlic paste*
1 tsp green chilli paste*
4 tbsp ghee*

STUFFING:
150g sattu (roasted black gram flour)*
50g red onion, finely chopped
2 green chillies, finely chopped
1 tbsp coriander leaves, finely chopped
1 tsp cumin seeds, toasted and crushed
½ tsp ajwain seeds
1 tsp finely chopped root ginger
½ tsp salt

TO SERVE:
melted ghee*, to dip or brush
cauliflower and potato curry (page 109)

KARJIKAI

Coorgi vegetable puffs KARNATAKA, SOUTH INDIA

Originating from Coorg, this is another samosa – with a difference in shape and spicing. Similar pastries are made all over India. These are particularly good served with a cucumber salad (page 32).

Sift the flour and salt into a bowl, add 90ml water and mix until smooth. Knead in the oil to make a pliable dough. Wrap in cling film and leave to rest in the fridge for 30 minutes.

For the stuffing, par-boil the potato in salted water for 5–7 minutes; drain, cool slightly and grate. Heat the oil in a pan and sauté the cumin seeds and curry leaves for 2 minutes. Add the chilli and ginger; sauté for 1 minute.

Add the carrots and beans and cook, stirring, for 3 minutes. Add the powdered spices and cook for 1 minute. Stir in the potato and peas and cook for 5–8 minutes until the vegetables are tender. Check seasoning.

Divide the dough into 12 balls and roll each piece to a round, 10cm in diameter. Put a generous spoonful of stuffing on one side of each round and moisten the dough edges with water. Fold the dough over the filling and press the edges together to seal. Rest the pastries for 15 minutes.

Heat the oil for deep-frying in a suitable pan to 170°C. Deep-fry the samosas, a few at a time, for 3–5 minutes or until golden. Serve hot.

200g strong plain flour
½ tsp salt
3 tbsp vegetable oil
vegetable oil, to deep-fry

STUFFING:
250g potato, peeled and quartered
salt
2 tbsp oil
½ tsp cumin seeds
6 curry leaves
1 green chilli, finely chopped
1 tbsp finely chopped root ginger
100g carrots, peeled and grated
50g French beans, cut into short lengths
½ tsp each ground coriander, turmeric
　and cumin
½ tsp red chilli powder
100g shelled fresh peas

LUQMI

Spicy lamb pastries HYDERABAD, SOUTH INDIA

The word *luqmi* is derived from the Arabic *luqma*, meaning a morsel. Serve with mango and passion fruit chutney (page 140).

Sift the flour and salt into a bowl, add the yogurt and 100ml water and mix until smooth. Knead in the ghee or oil to make a pliable dough. Wrap in cling film and leave to rest in the fridge for 30 minutes.

For the stuffing, put the mince, spices, ginger-garlic paste, salt and 500ml water in a pan. Bring to a simmer and cook for 30 minutes or until the lamb is cooked and the mixture is dry. Heat the oil in another pan and sauté the chillies and coriander for 1 minute. Add the mince and cook, stirring, for 3–5 minutes. Add the lemon zest and juice; take off the heat.

Divide the dough into 16 pieces. Roll out each one to an oblong, 15cm in length. Put 2 tbsp stuffing in the middle, moisten the dough edges with water and fold over to enclose the stuffing and form a rectangle, about 7.5 x 4cm. Press the edges well to seal and trim to neaten.

Heat the oil for deep-frying in a suitable pan to 170°C. Deep-fry the pastries a few at a time for 5–6 minutes until golden brown. Serve hot.

250g strong plain flour
1 tsp salt
2 tbsp yogurt
4 tbsp ghee* or vegetable oil
vegetable oil, to deep-fry

STUFFING:
500g lean lamb mince
1 tsp red chilli powder
½ tsp ground turmeric
1 tbsp ginger-garlic paste*
½ tsp salt
3 tbsp vegetable oil
4 green chillies, finely chopped
2 tbsp chopped coriander leaves
grated zest and juice of 2 lemons

NIZAMI SUBJ KATHI

Spicy vegetable wrap CALCUTTA, EAST INDIA

This is typical street food in Calcutta, but it is also an excellent snack or starter to prepare at home. The original version, created under Muslim rule in east India, featured meat pan-fried with spices and vegetables and then rolled in a large *roti* or flat bread. Often this bread was dipped into egg batter and pan-fried first, to keep it moist around the filling. I think my vegetarian version is equally exciting.

First make the filling. Heat the oil in a wok or kadhai, add the cumin seeds and sauté until they crackle. Add the ginger julienne, green chilli and onion. Sauté gently until the onion is softened and translucent. Add the carrot, cabbage and mushrooms and sauté for 1 minute. Add the powdered spices and salt, and cook for 2–3 minutes until the vegetables soften slightly. Add the paneer strips and toss to mix. Remove from the heat and allow to cool, then add the lemon juice and chopped coriander leaves.

To make the batter, put the gram flour, salt, spices and chopped coriander into a bowl and mix well. Add about 5–6 tbsp water and mix to a smooth, thick batter.

To cook the chapattis, heat the 3 tbsp oil in a large frying pan. One at a time, dip the chapattis into the batter and pan-fry for about 1 minute on each side.

To assemble, lay the breads on a clean surface, spoon the filling in to the centre and add some roasted pepper julienne. Roll up to enclose the filling. Serve the wraps warm or cold, garnished with coriander and accompanied by mint chutney and a salad (see below).

Cucumber and tomato salad: Toss julienne of cucumber, onion and tomato in lemon juice with a sprinkling of red chilli powder and toasted cumin seeds to serve with this wrap.

4 large chapattis or tortillas

3 tbsp vegetable oil

FILLING:

60ml vegetable oil

1 tsp cumin seeds

1 tsp root ginger julienne

1 tsp chopped green chilli

1 red onion, thinly sliced

1 carrot, cut into julienne

100g white cabbage, cut into julienne

50g shiitake mushrooms, sliced

1 tsp red chilli powder

1 tsp ground turmeric

1 tsp ground coriander

½ tsp garam masala

½ tsp salt, or to taste

100g paneer cheese, cut into strips

1 tbsp lemon juice

2 tbsp chopped coriander leaves

100g roasted (or grilled) red pepper,
      cut into julienne

BATTER:

50g gram flour*

¼ tsp salt

¼ tsp red chilli powder

¼ tsp ground turmeric

1 tbsp chopped coriander leaves

TO SERVE:

coriander sprigs, to garnish

mint chutney (page 140)

RAJMA KE GELAWATI

Red kidney bean cakes NORTH INDIA

I first ate these soft, savoury cakes in a strict vegetarian house in the city of Benares and was so impressed that I persuaded the family to let me have the recipe. It's an easy recipe with no-fuss ingredients, and the cakes taste superb.

Drain the kidney beans, put into a saucepan and add the cardamom pod and enough cold water to cover generously. Bring to the boil and boil steadily for 10 minutes, then lower the heat and cook for 1½ hours or until tender, adding salt towards the end of the cooking time.

Drain the beans and place in a blender or food processor with the cumin, chilli powder and coconut. Whiz until smooth, then tip into a bowl.

Add the mint, ginger and mango powder, and mix well. Finally mix in the breadcrumbs and check the seasoning, adding a little more salt if needed. Shape the mixture into cakes, 5cm in diameter and 1cm thick. Place on a tray and refrigerate for 30 minutes.

To cook the cakes, heat a non-stick frying pan or griddle, add the oil and lower the heat to medium. Fry the cakes for 3–4 minutes on each side until crisp and browned. Serve hot, with mustard and yogurt chutney.

250g dried red kidney beans, soaked in cold water overnight
1 black cardamom pod
1 tsp salt, or to taste
1½ tsp toasted cumin seeds, crushed
1 tsp red chilli powder
2 tbsp toasted unsweetened desiccated coconut*
2 tbsp chopped mint leaves
1 tbsp chopped root ginger
1 tsp mango powder*
2 tbsp fresh breadcrumbs
2 tbsp vegetable oil
mustard and yogurt chutney (page 138)

ALOO TIKKI

Pan-fried potato cakes LUCKNOW, NORTH INDIA

The gastronomic city of Lucknow is home to _Chowk ki Tikki_ – a street which is famous for its enticing food. During the Mogul empire, the _Nawab_ rulers of this city spent most of their time promoting art, culture and food, so Lucknow has a long tradition of courting food. It even has its own cuisine, called _awadhi_. These tasty potato cakes are best served with tomato chutney, but tomato ketchup will do if you are short of time.

Par-boil the potatoes in salted water for 5–7 minutes, then drain. When cool enough to handle, peel and grate, then place in a bowl.

Add the spices, ginger, green chilli and chopped coriander. Mix thoroughly and season with salt to taste.

Shape the mixture into cakes, 5cm in diameter and 1cm thick, and pat well to firm up. Place on a tray and refrigerate for 20 minutes.

To cook the cakes, heat a non-stick frying pan or griddle, add the oil and lower the heat to medium. Fry the cakes for 3–5 minutes on each side until crisp and browned. Serve hot, with tomato chutney.

400g potatoes, peeled and quartered
salt
1½ tsp toasted cumin seeds, crushed
½ tsp red chilli powder
1 tbsp chopped root ginger
½ tsp chopped green chilli
2 tbsp chopped coriander leaves
2 tbsp vegetable oil
tomato chutney, to serve (page 139)

SHAMMI KEBAB

Pan-fried lamb cakes   LUCKNOW, NORTH INDIA

The *Nawab* rulers of Lucknow favoured these lamb cakes with their interesting blend of meat, lentil and spices. The rulers of Hyderabad had their own version of *shammi*, called *shikampuri kebab*. The *Nawabs* created all manner of variations and spared no expense with their choice of flavourings. However, this is a simple recipe and one that works well. If you have kewra water* to hand, add 1 tsp to the mixture with the chopped herbs to enhance the flavour.

Put the lamb mince in a pan with the garlic, gram, dried chillies, whole spices, ½ tsp salt and 500ml water. Bring to the boil, lower the heat and simmer, uncovered, for about 40 minutes until the meat and gram are cooked and the water has evaporated. Cool slightly, then remove the whole spices if preferred. Put the mixture into a food processor or blender and whiz to a smooth, fine paste.

Tip the meat paste into a bowl and add the onions, ginger, green chillies and powdered spices. Mix thoroughly, add salt to taste, then add the chopped herbs and mix until evenly blended.

Divide the mixture into 14–18 pieces and shape into small round cakes. Place the lamb cakes on a tray and rest in the fridge for 30 minutes.

Heat the oil in a non-stick frying pan over a medium heat. Shallow-fry the lamb cakes, in batches, for about 2–3 minutes on each side. Serve hot, garnished with coriander sprigs. Accompany with mint chutney and mango chutney topped with some shredded mango.

500g lean lamb mince
5 garlic cloves, peeled
100g Bengal gram*
4 dried red chillies
6 black peppercorns
2 black cardamom pods
2.5cm cassia bark or cinnamon stick
1 tsp salt, or to taste
100g onions, finely chopped
1 tbsp finely chopped root ginger
5 green chillies, finely chopped
1 tsp garam masala
½ tsp ground mace
½ tsp green cardamom powder
2 tbsp chopped mint leaves
2 tbsp chopped coriander leaves
150ml vegetable oil, to shallow-fry

TO SERVE:
coriander sprigs, to garnish
mint chutney (page 140)
mango chutney (page 140)
a little shredded green mango

MURG KALEJI MASALA

Pan-fried chicken livers   PUNJAB, NORTH INDIA

Chicken livers are highly prized in Punjab – the equivalent to foie gras in France. In local villages a plate of pan-fried chicken livers is often served with drinks in the evening. I like to serve them in toasted poppadoms with a simple cucumber and tomato salad (page 20).

Cut the chicken livers into 2–3cm dice and set aside. Heat the oil in a sauté pan and sauté the cumin seeds until they crackle. Add the chopped ginger, then the onion and sauté until softened.

Add the chicken livers and sauté for 1 minute, then add the mushrooms and sauté for 2 minutes. Add the powdered spices and cook, stirring, for 30 seconds. Add the chopped tomatoes, season with salt and cook for 1 minute. Stir in the lime juice and remove from the heat.

Serve the chicken livers sprinkled with the chopped coriander leaves.

200g chicken livers, trimmed and cleaned
1 tbsp vegetable oil
1 tsp cumin seeds
1 tbsp finely chopped root ginger
50g onion, finely chopped
60g button mushrooms, quartered
¼ tsp ground turmeric
½ tsp red chilli powder
½ tsp ground coriander
1 small tomato, deseeded and chopped
½ tsp salt, or to taste
1 tbsp lime juice
1 tbsp chopped coriander leaves

PASTEIS DE OSTRAS

Oyster pasties GOA, WEST INDIA

In Goa, these pasties are filled with all manner of tasty stuffings – based on meat, fish or vegetables – and they are usually deep-fried rather than baked. I like to serve them with a tomato chutney, or a spicy tomato ketchup.

First make the stuffing. Heat the oil in a sauté pan and sauté the onion until softened. Add the ginger-garlic paste and sauté for 1–2 minutes, then add the green chillies and turmeric and sauté for another minute.

Add the peppers with the salt, and sauté until they have softened. Add the reserved oyster juice and white wine. Let bubble until the liquid has evaporated, then add the oysters and sauté for 1 minute. Remove from the heat and set aside to cool.

Preheat oven to 200°C (180°C fan oven) mark 6. Roll out the pastry to a 5mm thickness and cut out 4 rounds, 12cm in diameter, using a saucer as a guide. Spoon the oyster mixture on to one side of the rounds and brush the pastry edges with egg wash. Fold the pastry over the filling and press the edges together to seal and form pasties. Brush with egg wash and bake for 8–12 minutes until the pastry is risen and golden brown.

Serve warm, topped with spring onion julienne and accompanied by a tomato chutney, and a mixed leaf salad if you like.

375g pack puff pastry
1 small egg, beaten with 1 tsp water (egg wash)
100g mixed salad leaves

STUFFING:
1 tbsp vegetable oil
1 large onion, chopped
2 tsp ginger-garlic paste*
1 tsp chopped green chillies
½ tsp ground turmeric
60g chopped mixed red and yellow peppers
½ tsp salt
400g oysters, cleaned and shucked, juice reserved
2 tbsp white wine

TO SERVE:
spring onion julienne
tomato chutney (page 139)

FOFOS

Goan fish croquettes GOA, WEST INDIA

Introduced into Goa by the Portuguese, this recipe was originally made with salt cod. I normally use fresh cod or halibut, but you can use any fresh firm fish, or prawns if you prefer. Ideal party food.

Put the fish into a shallow pan with the fish stock and poach gently for about 10 minutes until just tender. Drain, reserving 3 tbsp stock, and flake the fish, removing any small residual bones. Par-boil the potato in salted water for 5–7 minutes, then drain and grate when cool enough to handle.

Put the fish, grated potato, onion, chilli, ginger, cumin seeds and chopped coriander into a bowl and mix well. Sprinkle in the cornflour and stir to mix. Moisten with the reserved fish stock and season with salt and pepper to taste. Add the egg yolk and mix well to combine. Divide the mixture into 16 pieces and shape into croquettes or rolls.

Heat the oil for deep-frying in a suitable pan to 180°C. Beat the egg white. Dip the fish rolls into the egg white, then deep-fry for 2 minutes or until golden; drain on kitchen paper. Serve hot, with the tomato chutney.

500g cod or halibut fillet
400ml fish stock, to poach
1 medium potato, peeled and quartered
salt and freshly ground black pepper
1 red onion, finely chopped
1 green chilli, chopped
1 tbsp chopped root ginger
1 tsp toasted cumin seeds
1 tbsp chopped coriander leaves
1½ tbsp cornflour
1 egg, separated
vegetable oil, to deep-fry

TO SERVE:
tomato chutney (page 139)

VAINGAN KATRI

Stuffed aubergine steaks GUJARAT, WEST INDIA

I have cooked this recipe with different regional influences, but this version from Gujarat is my favourite. Choose medium-sized aubergines – large steaks can be difficult to handle in the pan.

Cut 4 steaks from the widest part of the aubergine, each 2cm thick. Scoop out the pulp from the centres, leaving a 1cm border intact. Sprinkle with the salt and set aside for 30 minutes to degorge the bitter juices.

Meanwhile, make the stuffing. Cut the potatoes into even-sized pieces and par-boil in salted water for 5–7 minutes. Drain and leave until cool enough to handle, then grate finely.

Heat 3 tbsp oil in a sauté pan, wok or kadhai. Add the asafoetida and, as it sizzles, add the chopped garlic, green chilli and cumin seeds. Sauté for a minute or two until the garlic is light brown in colour and the cumin seeds crackle.

Add the grated carrots and cauliflower and sauté for 5 minutes, then stir in the ground coriander, chilli powder and turmeric. Sauté for 30 seconds. Add the grated potatoes, sugar, ginger and salt, and cook well for 12–15 minutes, then add the chopped coriander leaves. Remove from the heat and set aside.

Rinse the aubergine steaks carefully under cold running water and dry with kitchen paper. Place on a board and spoon the stuffing into the centres. Heat a thin film of oil in a non-stick frying pan. Using a fish slice, lift the stuffed aubergine steaks into the pan and fry for about 1½ minutes on each side until golden. Remove and drain on kitchen paper.

Serve warm, garnished with coriander sprigs and accompanied by mustard yogurt chutney.

400g aubergine
¼ tsp salt

STUFFING:
200g potatoes, peeled and quartered
salt
3 tbsp vegetable oil, plus
    extra to shallow-fry
pinch of asafoetida*
1 tsp chopped garlic
1 green chilli, chopped
1 tsp cumin seeds
50g carrots, grated
50g cauliflower, grated
2 tsp ground coriander
½ tsp red chilli powder
½ tsp ground turmeric
½ tsp raw sugar or jaggery*
1 tbsp chopped root ginger
3 tbsp chopped coriander leaves

TO SERVE:
coriander sprigs, to garnish
mustard and yogurt chutney (page 138)

TANDOORI PANEER AUR HARI GOBI

Roasted paneer and broccoli NORTH INDIA

Barbecues are a year-round event in India and many Punjabi villages have community tandoori ovens, where locals can take marinated meats or vegetables, and bread doughs to cook in the summer evenings or winter afternoons. This recipe is traditionally prepared with cauliflower, but I have used broccoli for colour. It works well in a domestic oven, or you can cook it on a barbecue.

First make the roux. Heat the oil in a heavy-based pan, add the gram flour and cook gently for about 3 minutes, stirring constantly; do not allow to burn. Take off the heat.

Cut the paneer into 4cm squares, 1cm thick, and place in a shallow dish. Put the ingredients for the paneer marinade into a bowl, add 2 tbsp of the gram flour roux and whisk together until smooth. Spoon over the paneer, turn to coat and set aside to marinate in a cool place for 2 hours.

Cut the broccoli into large florets and place in a bowl. Put the ingredients for the broccoli marinade in a blender or mini-processor with 1 tbsp of the gram flour roux and whiz until smooth. Spoon over the broccoli, turn to coat and set aside in a cool place to marinate for 1 hour.

Preheat oven to 200°C (180°C fan oven) mark 6. Put the paneer and broccoli in separate roasting trays. Roast in the hot oven for 8–12 minutes until the paneer cubes are golden brown on the surface and the broccoli is tender, basting occasionally with the oil and butter mix.

Arrange the roasted broccoli and paneer on warmed plates, sprinkle with the chaat masala and lime juice, and garnish with salad leaves and apple slices. Serve at once, with the mint chutney.

200g paneer cheese
250g broccoli
100ml oil and melted butter mix, to baste

ROUX:
3 tbsp vegetable oil
3 tbsp gram flour*

PANEER MARINADE:
100g yogurt
30ml double cream
1 tsp garam masala
1 tsp ground coriander
1 tsp ground turmeric
½ tsp red chilli powder
2 tbsp mint leaves, finely chopped
1 tbsp finely chopped root ginger
1 tsp toasted cumin seeds, crushed
¼ tsp powdered saffron

BROCCOLI MARINADE:
30g garlic cloves, peeled
50g Cheddar cheese, grated
4 green chillies, roughly chopped
½ tsp salt
100ml double cream

TO SERVE:
½ tsp chaat masala*, or to taste
lime juice, to sprinkle
salad leaves and apple slices, to garnish
mint chutney (page 140)

TANDOORI SUBJ CHAAT

Roasted vegetable salad NORTH INDIA

**With a population that is 80% vegetarian, Indian cuisine boasts a
wealth of interesting vegetarian dishes. Grilling or roasting vegetables
and fruits in a tandoor is common practice in northern India. Here
I have used the grill, but you could cook the skewers on a barbecue
if you prefer. Serve them on the skewers, or rest for a few minutes,
then transfer to a bowl and toss with a handful of mixed salad leaves
and carrot and mooli (daikon) julienne, as illustrated. Serve with mint
chutney (page 140).**

First, prepare the marinade. Put all the ingredients into a bowl and mix
together thoroughly.

Halve, core and deseed the red peppers, then cut into 4cm pieces.
Cut the star fruit into 1cm thick slices. Quarter and core the apples and
pear, then cut into 4cm chunks. Cut the banana into 4cm chunks.

Add all the fruits and vegetables to the marinade, including the onion.
Toss well to mix. If using paneer, cut into 4cm squares and add to the
bowl. Set aside to marinate in a cool place for 30 minutes.

Preheat the grill to medium-high. Thread the vegetables, fruit and
paneer if using, alternately on to kebab skewers. Grill, turning occasionally,
for 5–7 minutes or until lightly charred.

Serve hot, sprinkled with chaat masala and lime juice.

2 red peppers
1 star fruit
1 red apple
1 Granny Smith apple
1 pear
1 banana
1 small red onion, peeled and thinly sliced
100g paneer cheese (optional)

MARINADE:
3 tbsp lime juice, plus extra to sprinkle
1 tbsp toasted cumin seeds, crushed
1 tsp crushed red chilli flakes
1 tbsp chaat masala*, plus extra to sprinkle
1 tsp pomegranate seed powder*
½ tsp salt, or to taste
100g blanched almonds, crushed
150g natural set yogurt
1 tbsp chopped green chillies
2 tbsp chopped root ginger
3 tbsp vegetable oil

VELLARIKKAI KOSUMALLI

Cucumber salad TAMIL NADU, SOUTH INDIA

**This is a typical south Indian salad – lightly seasoned, highly nutritious
and a perfect cooler in a scorching climate. It is an excellent appetiser
and a good accompaniment for most main meals.
(Illustrated on page 18)**

Halve the cucumber lengthways and scoop out the seeds, then cut into
long julienne and place in a bowl. Add the sprouted beans, coconut, chilli,
chopped coriander, lemon zest and juice, and salt. Toss the ingredients
together to mix and set aside.

Heat the oil in a sauté pan, and add the mustard seeds, black and
Bengal gram, asafoetida, crushed dried chilli and curry leaves. Sauté for
1–2 minutes until the spices splutter, then add to the salad and mix well.
Serve chilled.

1 large thin-skinned cucumber
2 tbsp mixed sprouted beans
2 tbsp grated fresh coconut*
1 green chilli, chopped
2 tbsp coriander leaves, chopped
grated zest and juice of 1 lemon
¼ tsp salt, or to taste
2 tsp vegetable oil
1 tsp mustard seeds
1 tsp each black and Bengal gram*
¼ tsp asafoetida*
½ tsp crushed dried red chilli
8 curry leaves

SUNDAL

Chickpea, mango and coconut salad TAMIL NADU, SOUTH INDIA

Sundal is a tasty salad and a street food snack, which is particularly popular on the beaches in Chennai. The ingredients are often varied – dried green peas or other beans may replace chickpeas, peanuts are sometimes added, and other fruits may be used instead of mango.

Drain the chickpeas and put into a saucepan with 1 litre fresh water. Bring to the boil, reduce the heat and simmer until the chickpeas are cooked, about 2 hours. Season with ½ tsp salt after 1¾ hours. Drain the chickpeas.

Heat the oil in a sauté pan. Add the mustard seeds and gram, and sauté for a minute or two until the mixture splutters, then add the red chilli, asafoetida and curry leaves, and sauté for another minute.

Add the cooked chickpeas and sauté for 2–3 minutes, then remove from the heat. Add the coconut, chilli, mango julienne, chopped plums if using, and lemon zest and juice. Toss to mix all the salad ingredients together and check the seasoning. Finally, add the chopped coriander.

Serve warm or cold, garnished with mango slices and coriander sprigs.

250g chickpeas, soaked in cold water overnight
½ tsp salt, or to taste
2 tsp groundnut oil
1 tsp mustard seeds
1 tsp black gram*
1 dried red chilli
¼ tsp asafoetida*
1 tsp chopped curry leaves
2 tbsp grated fresh coconut*
1 green chilli, finely chopped
½ green mango, peeled and cut into julienne, plus slices to garnish
2 plums, stoned and chopped (optional)
grated zest and juice of 1 lemon
1 tbsp chopped coriander leaves, plus sprigs to garnish

JAL TARANG

Scallop and tiger prawn salad EAST INDIA

I created this recipe for my restaurant and it is one of my favourites. It is a light, wholesome medley of shellfish, fruit and salad ingredients with east Indian spicing techniques.

Peel and de-vein the prawns; remove the coral from the scallops. Rinse the shellfish, pat dry and set aside.

For the dressing, blend all the ingredients together in a blender or food processor until smooth; set aside until needed.

Heat the oil in a sauté pan, add the sesame, nigella and ajwain seeds and sauté for 2 minutes until they crackle. Add the paprika and ginger, and sauté until the ginger releases its aroma.

Add the prawns and sauté for 3–4 minutes until they are almost cooked; remove to a bowl and set aside. Add the scallops to the pan and cook for 1 minute until lightly caramelised, then turn them and cook on the other side for 1 minute; remove and add to the prawns with half of the dressing. Toss to mix and leave for 2 minutes to allow the flavours to be absorbed. Meanwhile, toss the root vegetable julienne and rocket leaves in 1 tbsp of the dressing. Arrange the salad and seafood in a large deep plate and sprinkle with the toasted pumpkin and poppy seeds. Serve the rest of the dressing separately.

16 raw tiger prawns
12 large scallops, cleaned
20ml olive or vegetable oil
½ tsp each sesame, nigella seeds and ajwain seeds
¼ tsp paprika
1 tbsp root ginger julienne
handful of mixed carrot, mooli (daikon) and beetroot julienne
handful of wild baby rocket leaves
1 tbsp pumpkin seeds, lightly toasted
1 tbsp mixed black and white poppy seeds, toasted

DRESSING:
200g mixed black and green seedless grapes
50g mint leaves
20g root ginger, roughly chopped
2 small green chillies, roughly chopped
½ tsp salt, or to taste
1 tsp mango powder or chaat masala*
20ml olive oil or vegetable oil

JHINGA TIL TINKA

Deep-fried prawns with vermicelli coating NORTH INDIA

These crunchy coated, juicy prawns are delicious with apple chutney (page 141) as an appetiser. Alternatively, you can serve them as a starter with a light cucumber and tomato salad (page 20), or use to garnish fresh crab salad (as illustrated).

Peel and de-vein the prawns, leaving the tail shells intact; wash and pat dry with kitchen paper. Put all the ingredients for the marinade in a bowl and mix together thoroughly. Add the prawns, turn to coat and set aside in a cool place to marinate for 45 minutes.

Mix together the sesame seeds and vermicelli on a plate, for the coating. Remove the prawns from the marinade and coat liberally with the vermicelli mixture, pressing with your fingers to ensure it adheres. Leave the prawns to rest for 5 minutes.

Heat the oil for deep-frying in a suitable pan to 180°C. Deep-fry the prawns, a few at a time, for 2–3 minutes until the coating is golden brown and crunchy. Serve with apple chutney or salad, or use to garnish the crab salad (below).

8 king prawns

2 tbsp sesame seeds

50g vermicelli

vegetable oil, to deep-fry

MARINADE:

2 garlic cloves, crushed

½ tsp red chilli powder

grated zest and juice of 1 lemon

3 tbsp yogurt

1 tbsp chopped root ginger

30g Cheddar cheese, grated

1 tsp ajwain seeds

2 tbsp single cream

1 tbsp gram flour*, toasted

¼ tsp green cardamom powder

1 tsp salt

SALADA DE CARANGUEJOS

Crab salad with coconut and curry leaves GOA, WEST INDIA

All around the Indian coast, there are spectacular shellfish dishes. Preparation and spicing techniques vary with the locality, but curry leaves, fresh coconut, green chillies and mustard seeds are almost always present. In Goa, this salad is prepared with native blue crabs, but any freshly prepared white crab meat will do.

Heat the oil in a wok, add the mustard seeds and sauté until they splutter, then add the curry leaves and sauté for a minute or two. Add the ginger and green chillies and cook, stirring, for 2 minutes.

Add the chopped onions and sauté until softened and translucent. Add the crab meat, stir for a few seconds, then add the turmeric and salt. Sauté for 2 minutes, then stir in the coconut milk, grated coconut and chopped coriander. Remove from the heat and allow to cool.

Serve the salad cold, with kumquat or mango and passion fruit chutney.

Variation: For a special presentation (as illustrated), shape the salad neatly using metal rings. Serve each portion topped with a crisp-fried coated prawn (see above) and a sprig of coriander.

3 tbsp vegetable oil or coconut oil

1½ tsp mustard seeds

10 curry leaves, finely chopped

1 tsp finely chopped root ginger

½ tsp finely chopped green chillies

100g onions, finely chopped

300g white crab meat, flaked

1 tsp ground turmeric

½ tsp salt, or to taste

3 tbsp coconut milk*

1 tbsp grated fresh coconut*

1 tsp chopped coriander leaves

TO SERVE:

kumquat chutney (page 141), or mango and
  passion fruit chutney (page 140)

FISH AND SHELLFISH

With almost 8000km of coastline and warm seas, India is blessed with some of the most exotic fish and seafood in the world. There are fish stalls in almost every coastal village, with huge fish markets in major fishing towns. From Mumbai all around the coast to Calcutta, I have sampled some of the most exquisite fish and shellfish preparations in coastal homes and fishermen's shacks. Travelling around the coast is a real gastronomic experience because preparation and cooking techniques for fish vary so much from one state to another, as you will discover in this chapter.

MEEN MOLEE

Coconut fish curry KERALA, SOUTH INDIA

This recipe from coastal Kerala combines fresh ingredients in a simple way. It is a prime example of India's minimalist cooking.

Remove any small bones from the fish fillets with tweezers. Mix ½ tsp salt with 1 tsp turmeric and gently rub into the fish fillets.

Heat the coconut oil in a wide pan. Add the onions, chillies and garlic, and sauté for a few minutes, then add the curry leaves and keep cooking until the onion is translucent. Take out half of the curry leaves and set aside for the garnish.

Add the rest of the turmeric and salt to the pan. Pour in the coconut milk and heat through, then add the fish fillets and simmer very gently for 3–4 minutes until just cooked. Serve immediately, garnished with the reserved curry leaves and coriander.

4 small sea bass fillets, each about 150g

1 tsp salt, or to taste

1½ tsp ground turmeric

2 tbsp coconut oil

2 medium onions, finely sliced

6 green chillies, slit lengthways

3 garlic cloves, sliced into fine strips

20 curry leaves

400ml coconut milk*

coriander sprigs, to garnish

HARI MACHCHI

John Dory fried in green spice paste EAST INDIA

I developed this dish while working at the Oberoi hotel in Orissa. I like my flavours to be simple and straightforward and I have always been partial to easy cooking. This recipe is very close to my heart.

Put the fish fillets in a shallow dish, sprinkle with the lemon juice and salt, and leave to marinate for 15 minutes.

Meanwhile, put the ingredients for the green spice paste in a blender or mini-processor and whiz to a fairly smooth paste.

Pat the fish dry with kitchen paper and coat liberally with the green spice paste, massaging it over the fillets with your fingers. Leave to marinate in the fridge for 40 minutes. In the meantime, wash the spinach, drain well and cut into julienne. Pat dry thoroughly, with kitchen paper.

Heat the oil in a shallow frying pan. Remove the excess marinade from the fish, then place the fillets flesh-side down in the pan and fry for 2 minutes. Turn the fish over and fry skin-side down for 2–3 minutes or until just cooked.

Meanwhile, heat the oil for deep-frying in a deep-fryer or other deep pan to 180°C and deep-fry the spinach in small batches for 30 seconds or so until crisp. Remove the spinach with a slotted spoon as it stops crackling and drain on kitchen paper.

When the fish is cooked, remove and drain on kitchen paper. Serve on warmed plates topped with the fried spinach, sprinkled with chaat masala.

4 John Dory fillets, each about 150g

2 tbsp lemon juice

½ tsp salt

4 tbsp vegetable oil

GREEN SPICE PASTE:

50g mint leaves

50g coriander leaves

10g root ginger, chopped

2 green chillies, stems removed

1½ tsp dried fenugreek leaf powder*

2 tsp chaat masala*

1 tsp red chilli powder

½ tsp salt

2 tbsp gram flour*

DEEP-FRIED SPINACH:

200g spinach leaves

vegetable oil, to deep-fry

1 tsp chaat masala*

MEEN DAKSHINI

Deccan fish curry   ANDHRA PRADESH, SOUTH INDIA

This tangy fish curry has a perfectly balanced combination of south Indian flavours. Red mullet is a good alternative to the *murrel* fish used in Andhra Pradesh. The cuisine of this state is very spicy, but if you have an antidote of a yogurt drink with your meal, you will be fine!

Slice the fish crossways, through the bone, to give steaks about 4cm wide; discard the heads if you wish. Mix together the ginger-garlic paste, salt, chilli powder and turmeric. Rub gently into the fish and leave to marinate in the fridge for at least 30 minutes. Meanwhile, soak the tamarind pulp in 200ml warm water for 20 minutes, then strain through a fine sieve.

Heat the oil in a frying pan and fry 10 curry leaves until crisp; remove and set aside for the garnish. Add the cumin and mustard seeds to the pan and fry until they begin to crackle. Add the onions and remaining curry leaves, and fry until the onions are softened and golden brown.

Add the fish and chillies, and fry lightly until the chillies have softened, turning once. Add the tamarind liquid and simmer gently for 3–5 minutes until the fish is cooked. Serve sprinkled with the fried curry leaves and chopped coriander. Accompany with Indian bread or steamed rice.

4 small red mullet, each about 300g, scaled
  and cleaned
2 tsp ginger-garlic paste*
1/2 tsp salt
1 tsp chilli powder
1/4 tsp ground turmeric
1 tbsp tamarind pulp*
3 tbsp sunflower or vegetable oil
20 curry leaves
1 tsp cumin seeds
1/2 tsp black mustard seeds
2 medium onions, finely sliced
4 green chillies, finely sliced
chopped coriander leaves, to garnish

DOI MAACH

Spiced fish with yogurt   BENGAL, EAST INDIA

Anything *doi* or *jhole* is Bengali and this recipe epitomises Bengali cuisine. The fish is cooked in yogurt, which splits as it is heated – a characteristic of this dish. Carp is the traditional choice, but you can use John Dory, cod, sole, red mullet or almost any other fish.

Put the fish fillets in a shallow dish, sprinkle with 1/4 tsp turmeric, 1/4 tsp salt, the ginger-garlic paste and lemon juice, and leave to marinate in the fridge for about 20 minutes.

Take out the fish and dust lightly with gram flour. Heat the oil in a shallow frying pan and pan-fry the fillets briefly for about 1 minute each side until golden brown in colour. Remove with a fish slice and set aside.

Add the bay leaf and whole spices to the pan and fry for 1–2 minutes. Add the onion and sauté until it is softened and brown. Add the remaining 1/4 tsp turmeric and the chilli powder, stir for 20–30 seconds, then add the yogurt, remaining salt and 100ml water. Bring to a simmer, stirring.

Add the fried fish pieces and simmer for 3 minutes or until the fish is cooked. Remove from the heat and sprinkle with the Bengali garam masala and chopped coriander. Serve with boiled rice.

4 John Dory or Dover sole fillets, each about 150g
1/2 tsp ground turmeric
1/2 tsp salt
1/2 tsp ginger-garlic paste*
1/2 tsp lemon juice
1 tbsp gram flour*, to dust
2 tbsp vegetable oil
1 bay leaf
1/2 tsp coriander seeds
1 dried red chilli
2 cloves
2 green cardamom pods
5cm cassia bark or cinnamon stick
1 medium onion, finely chopped
1 tsp red chilli powder
300g natural yogurt, lightly whisked
Bengali garam masala*, to sprinkle
1 tsp chopped coriander leaves

TENGA

Sweet and sour fish curry ASSAM, EAST INDIA

Red snapper steaks make this an Assamese curry with a difference. The original recipe featured *rohu* – a variety of carp found in the river Brahmaputra. Assam produces spices like turmeric, aniseed and galangal, and its proximity to Myanmar explains the use of Far Eastern ingredients, such as lime leaves, star anise and bamboo shoots. Here, canned bamboo shoots are used, but fermented bamboo shoot, known as *kharisa*, is more likely to be used in Assam.

Put the fish steaks in a shallow dish. Combine the ingredients for the marinade and rub all over the fish steaks. Set aside in a cool place to marinate for 30 minutes.

Heat the oil in a large frying pan, add the fish steaks and fry for about 1 minute on each side until lightly coloured. Remove the fish to a plate, and keep aside.

For the sauce, add the star anise, nigella and fennel seeds to the oil remaining in the pan and sauté for a few minutes until the spices splutter. Add the onions and sauté until softened and golden brown in colour.

Add the powdered spices, sauté for a minute, then add the salt, sugar and bamboo shoots. Add the lime leaves, lemon juice and 200ml water. Bring to the boil and simmer for a few minutes.

Return the fish steaks to the pan and add the sliced tomato. Cook for 7–8 minutes until the fish is tender, then add the chopped coriander. Serve garnished with sprigs of coriander.

4 red snapper steaks, each about 150g
100ml vegetable oil

MARINADE:
1 tsp finely chopped root ginger
½ tsp red chilli powder
½ tsp ground turmeric
1 tsp fennel seed powder
grated zest and juice of 1 lemon
½ tsp salt
1½ tsp palm sugar or jaggery*

SAUCE:
1 star anise
1 tsp nigella or onion seeds
1 tsp fennel seed or aniseed
2 medium onions, finely sliced
1½ tsp ground turmeric
1 tsp red chilli powder
½ tsp fennel powder
½ tsp salt, or to taste
1 tbsp palm sugar or jaggery*
100g bamboo shoots, sliced
3–4 lime leaves
2 tbsp lemon juice
1 large tomato, sliced
1 tbsp coriander leaves, chopped, plus extra
    sprigs to garnish

AMBOT-TIK

Konkani hot and sour fish stew   GOA, WEST INDIA

This spicy fish curry can be made with any firm-fleshed fish, such as swordfish, shark or monkfish. It is a very popular way of serving fish in west India. I like to garnish this dish with mustard and cress, but you could use ginger julienne if you prefer.

Cut the swordfish into 3cm cubes and set aside. Put the tamarind pulp in a bowl, pour on 100ml warm water and leave to soak for 20 minutes, then strain through a fine sieve.

Meanwhile, put the ingredients for the chilli paste in a blender or mini-processor and whiz to a fairly smooth paste.

Heat the oil in a saucepan, add the onions and fry gently for about 10 minutes until softened and browned. Add the chilli paste and sauté for 5 minutes, then add the tamarind liquid, stirring well. Bring the sauce to the boil and simmer for a minute.

Add the fish cubes and stir to coat in the sauce. Simmer gently for about 5–6 minutes or until just cooked. Check the seasoning, adding salt to taste. Serve garnished with mustard cress and lime slices. Accompany with boiled rice.

450g swordfish fillet
30g tamarind pulp*
2 tbsp vegetable oil
200g onions, finely sliced
½ tsp salt, or to taste

CHILLI PASTE:
10ml vinegar
6 dried red chillies
6 black peppercorns
1 tsp ground turmeric
1 tbsp ginger-garlic paste*
½ tsp cumin seeds
1 tsp sugar

GARNISH:
mustard cress
lime slices

ISMAILI MACHCHI CURRY

Khoja fish curry   WEST INDIA

The Khoja community in India have their own distinctive cuisine, which is quite different from popular Muglai food. Followers of the Ismaili branch of the Shia sect of Islam, they came to India from Iran, first landing at Gujarat. A strong Gujarati influence is evident in their food, but Khoja dishes maintain their own identity and they are a real treat. For this recipe, use firm-fleshed fish, like kingfish or monkfish.

Cut the fish into 1cm thick slices and place in a shallow dish. Sprinkle with the lemon juice and salt, and leave to marinate for 20 minutes.

Soak the tamarind pulp in 200ml warm water for 20 minutes, then strain through a fine sieve. Put the ingredients for the coconut spice paste in a blender or mini-processor and whiz to a fine paste.

Heat the oil in a saucepan, add the curry leaves and mustard seeds, and sauté until they crackle. Add the turmeric and coconut spice paste and sauté for 2 minutes or until the fat separates from the paste.

Add the fish and tamarind liquid, and bring to a simmer. Cook over a low heat for about 5 minutes until the fish is just cooked. Serve topped with chillies and chopped coriander. Accompany with rice or bread.

450g kingfish or monkfish fillet
1 tsp lemon juice
½ tsp salt
1 tbsp tamarind pulp*
2 tbsp vegetable oil
10 curry leaves
1 tsp black mustard seeds
½ tsp ground turmeric

COCONUT SPICE PASTE:
80g grated fresh coconut*
10 peppercorns
4 dried red chillies
6 garlic cloves, peeled

GARNISH:
3 green chillies, slit lengthways
2 tbsp chopped coriander leaves

NADIR GADH

Fish curry with lotus stems   KASHMIR, NORTH INDIA

Kashmiri cooking is unique because the spice pastes, nuts, fruits and flowers used for flavour, aroma and colour are uncommon in other regions. Here, the flavours are punchy, though the spicing is subtle. Fresh lotus stems are sometimes obtainable from Asian or Chinese food stores, but you can always substitute canned lotus stems. I have used red mullet, but trout works equally well.

Put the fish fillets in a shallow dish, sprinkle with the lemon juice and ½ tsp salt, and leave to marinate for 20 minutes. Meanwhile, whiz the onions in a blender or food processor to a fine paste.

Heat the oil in a frying pan, add the fish fillets and fry for 1 minute on each side until lightly coloured. Remove to a plate, and keep aside.

Add the garlic and sauté for 30 seconds, then add the lotus stems and fry for 2 minutes. Add the chilli powder and raw onion paste, and sauté for 3–5 minutes until light brown in colour.

Add the cloves, cardamom pods, ginger, turmeric, cassia or cinnamon, salt and fried onion paste. Pour in 500ml water, stir well and bring to the boil. Lower heat and simmer for 10 minutes until the lotus stems are tender.

Add the fish and infused saffron, and simmer gently for 2–3 minutes. Serve sprinkled with toasted cumin seeds and garnished with coriander.

450g red mullet fillets, with skin

1 tsp lemon juice

1 tsp salt, or to taste

100g onions, quartered

100ml vegetable oil

1 tbsp finely chopped garlic

120g lotus stems, sliced

1 tsp red chilli powder

3 cloves

5 green cardamom pods

2 black cardamom pods

1 tsp ground ginger

1½ tsp ground turmeric

2.5cm cassia bark or cinnamon stick

50g fried onion paste*

pinch of saffron threads, infused in 2 tbsp
   warm water

½ tsp toasted cumin seeds, crushed

coriander sprigs, to garnish

NIMBUWALI MACHCHI

Tandoori salmon with lime marinade   SOUTH INDIA

Cooking fish in a tandoor barbecue is very common in India. This is a popular barbecue recipe in the coastal town of Mangalore, where citrus flavours are well liked. It's a great way to spice up salmon.

Cut the salmon into 4cm large cubes, retaining the skin, and place in a shallow dish.

Put the garlic, coriander, ginger, lime zest and juice, lime leaves, chilli powder and garam masala in a blender or mini-processor and whiz to a fine paste. Heat the oil in a small pan, add the gram flour and cook, stirring, for 1–2 minutes to make a roux, without browning.

Mix the roux with the spice paste, salt and yogurt until smooth. Coat the salmon pieces with the mixture and leave to marinate for 1 hour.

Preheat the oven to 200°C (180°C fan oven) mark 6, or the grill or barbecue. Put the salmon on a rack (over a roasting tin if oven-cooking) and cook for 10–15 minutes, basting once or twice with butter to keep the fish moist. Serve the salmon hot, accompanied by a seasonal salad.

400g thick-cut salmon fillet

2 tbsp melted butter, to baste

MARINADE:

20 garlic cloves

small bunch of coriander, leaves only

1 knob of root ginger, lightly crushed

1 tbsp finely grated lime zest

2 tbsp lime juice

4–5 lime leaves

1 tsp red chilli powder

½ tsp garam masala

50ml vegetable oil

1 tbsp gram flour*

½ tsp salt

100g yogurt

MACHER DIYE CHAR DALER KHECHURI

Monkfish kedgeree   BENGAL, EAST INDIA

This recipe may look complicated, but in reality it is simple. Kedgeree is one of the culinary imports from India that often appears on our menus. In India, almost every state has its own version. *Elis hilsa* is the local catch used, but any firm-fleshed fish will do; of course, vegetarians can simply leave it out altogether. In eastern India, kedgeree is traditionally served with a range of accompaniments, including pickles, ghee, poppadoms, rice crisps and yogurt. If preferred the recipe can be simplified by using rice and just one type of lentil, in a 2:1 ratio.

Cut the monkfish into 1cm thick slices. Put half of these into a shallow dish and sprinkle with the lemon juice, red chilli powder, turmeric and ½ tsp salt. Turn to coat and set aside in a cool place to marinate for 30 minutes.

Meanwhile, bring 500ml water to the boil in a shallow pan and add 1 cassia or cinnamon stick, 2 cloves, 1 bay leaf and ½ tsp chopped ginger. Add the other 4 monkfish slices and poach for about 10 minutes until tender, then remove with a slotted spoon and set aside, reserving the poaching liquid.

Put the red lentils, split peas and split Bengal gram in a saucepan with the grated coconut. Add the reserved poaching liquid, 300ml water and 1 tsp salt. Simmer for about 20–25 minutes until cooked and soft. Drain.

Heat the butter in a separate pan and sauté the remaining cloves, cassia or cinnamon stick, bay leaves, ginger, cumin seeds and dried red chillies for 1 minute. Add the rice and moong lentils. Stir, then add 1 tsp salt, the sugar and 400ml water to cover the mixture. Bring to the boil, then lower the heat and simmer for about 20 minutes until the rice and lentils are cooked and all the liquid is absorbed. Meanwhile, flake the poached monkfish with a fork.

In a separate pan, heat the oil and fry the marinated pieces of fish for about 6–8 minutes until crisp and golden brown on the surface, and cooked through to the centre.

With a fork, mix together the rice, boiled lentils, poached monkfish and chopped coriander. Serve the kedgeree hot, topped with the fried monkfish pieces, coriander sprigs and a spoonful of coriander and peanut chutney.

Coriander and peanut chutney: Whiz 100g coriander leaves, 50g mint leaves, 35g toasted peanuts, 10g chopped root ginger, 1 green chilli, 2 tbsp lemon juice, 1 tsp salt and 1 tbsp water together in a blender or mini-processor to make a paste. Check the seasoning.

200g monkfish fillet

1 tsp lemon juice

½ tsp red chilli powder

½ tsp ground turmeric

salt

2 x 2.5cm cassia bark or cinnamon sticks

6 cloves

3 bay leaves

20g root ginger, chopped

30g dried red split lentils

30g dried split peas

30g dried split Bengal gram*

70g grated fresh coconut*

25g butter

1 tsp cumin seeds

2 dried red chillies

150g short-grain risotto rice

30g roasted moong lentils

½ tsp sugar

1½ tbsp vegetable oil

1 tbsp coriander leaves, chopped

coriander sprigs, to garnish

TO SERVE:

coriander and peanut chutney (see left)

SANDHNO NO PATIO

Jumbo prawn curry GUJARAT, WEST INDIA

This recipe takes its name from the pan or *patio* it is cooked in.
The best prawn *patio* recipe comes from Bharuch, an old Parsi town
on the banks of the River Narmada. This unique town was the first
hold of the Parsi community in India and boasts an 800-year-old fire
temple. Parsi cuisine is a good blend of Iranian and Indian ingredients.
If you cannot find fresh fenugreek leaves for this recipe, use chopped
spinach leaves instead.

Peel and de-vein the prawns, leaving the tail attached. Rinse and pat dry.
Next prepare the green spice paste. Put all the ingredients in a blender or
mini-processor and whiz to a fine paste. Spread half of the paste all over
the prawns and set aside to marinate for 30 minutes.

Heat half of the vegetable and sesame seed oils in a *patio* or deep
sauté pan. Add the remaining spice paste and sauté gently for 2 minutes.
Add the chopped onions and sauté until translucent, then add the rest of
the ingredients (except the prawns).

Heat the remaining oil in a separate sauté pan and fry the marinated
prawns for 1–2 minutes. Add the prawns to the onion mixture and simmer
for about 5 minutes until they are cooked. Serve at once.

8–12 jumbo raw prawns
2 tbsp vegetable oil
1 tbsp sesame seed oil
2 large onions, finely chopped
1/2 tsp salt
2 tsp chopped garlic
1 tsp ground turmeric
2 bunches of fenugreek leaves, stems removed
1 tbsp dried fenugreek leaves
2 tbsp coriander leaves
1 bunch of spring onions, trimmed and sliced

GREEN SPICE PASTE:
3 green chillies, stems removed
50g coriander leaves and stems
1 tsp ground turmeric
3 dried red chillies, halved and deseeded
1 tsp cumin seeds
1 tsp black peppercorns

ROYYALU PULUSU

Prawn curry ANDHRA PRADESH, SOUTH INDIA

I once thought that everything from southern India came from
Madras. When I was sent south for my education, I was amazed
at the colours, architecture, cuisine, religion and culture. It was so
varied and different from the robust north. I picked up this recipe
from a friend's mother in the coastal town of Kakinada.

Peel and de-vein the prawns, leaving the tail attached. Rinse and pat dry.
Mix together the mango powder, turmeric, chilli powder and salt, then rub
over the prawns and leave to marinate in a cool place for 20 minutes or so.

Heat the oil in a pan and sauté the onions until softened and golden.
Add the ginger-garlic paste and cook well for 2–3 minutes.

Add the ground coriander, cumin, grated coconut, green chillies,
pepper, mint and curry leaves, and sauté gently for 2–3 minutes.

Add the prawns and sauté for 1 minute. Pour in the coconut milk and
simmer for 5 minutes, then add the chopped tomatoes and 100ml water.
Simmer over a low heat for 4–5 minutes until the prawns are just cooked.

Scatter with chopped coriander and serve with chapattis or boiled rice.

300g medium raw prawns (about 16)
1/2 tsp mango powder*
1/4 tsp ground turmeric
1/4 tsp red chilli powder
1/2 tsp salt
60ml sesame seed oil
4 medium onions, sliced
2 tsp ginger-garlic paste*
1 tsp each ground coriander and cumin
100g grated fresh coconut*
2 green chillies, chopped
1/2 tsp crushed peppercorns
1 tbsp chopped mint leaves
1 tsp chopped curry leaves
250ml coconut milk*
2 tomatoes, chopped
2 tbsp chopped coriander leaves

CHEMEEN MANGA CHARU

Prawn and green mango curry KERALA, SOUTH INDIA

This dish comes from the Moplah Muslims of Kerala, a community descended from 7th century Arabs. Its fragrant mix of coconut, curry leaves and fresh seafood is typical of Kerala.

Peel and de-vein the prawns, leaving the tail attached. Rinse and pat dry.

Heat 1 tbsp coconut oil in a pan, add the coconut, chopped onion and fennel seeds, and sauté over a medium heat until the coconut is golden brown. Remove and grind to a smooth paste, using a blender.

Heat 2 tbsp coconut oil in the pan. Add the sliced onion and fry until translucent. Add the green chillies with the ginger-garlic paste, and sauté for 2–3 minutes. Stir in the ground spices and half the mango strips.

Add the prawns to the pan with the salt and cook, stirring, until they are opaque and almost cooked. Stir in the coconut paste, coconut milk and the rest of the mango. Simmer gently until the prawns are just cooked.

Meanwhile, heat the remaining 1 tbsp coconut oil in a separate pan and sauté the fenugreek seeds, mustard seeds and curry leaves until aromatic. Serve the prawn curry topped with the aromatic spice mixture and green mango strips. Accompany with rice or Indian bread.

300g large raw prawns (about 16)
4 tbsp coconut oil
70g grated fresh coconut*
½ onion, finely chopped
1 tsp fennel seeds
1 onion, finely sliced
2 green chillies, chopped
1½ tsp garlic-ginger paste*
1½ tsp ground coriander
1 tsp chilli powder
½ tsp ground turmeric
100g green mango, sliced into thin strips, plus extra to garnish
½ tsp salt, or to taste
200ml coconut milk*
1 tsp fenugreek seeds
1 tsp black mustard seeds
25 curry leaves

MOCHHA CHINGRI MAACHHER MOLAI CURRY

Lobster curry with coconut BENGAL, EAST INDIA

Everything is dramatic in Bengal, including this preparation with its impeccable spicing and flavouring. Rock or deep-sea lobster would be used in this part of India, but consider any lobster suitable.

Split the lobsters in two lengthways, clean and smear with the turmeric and ½ tsp salt. Process the onions in a blender or food processor to a paste.

Heat the oil in a deep sauté pan. Add the lobsters and sauté lightly for 2 minutes or until the shells colour; remove and set aside. Add the potatoes to the pan and sauté for a few minutes until golden. Remove and set aside.

Heat the ghee or butter in a saucepan and sauté the bay leaves, cloves, cassia or cinnamon and cardamom pods for 1–2 minutes. Add the onion paste and cook for 3–4 minutes until lightly cooked. Add the chilli and ginger-garlic pastes and sauté for a further 2 minutes until the masala is well cooked, adding a little water from time to time to keep it moist.

Add the potatoes with ½ tsp salt and the sugar. Pour in half the coconut milk and bring to a simmer. Add the lobster and simmer for 10 minutes. Add the rest of the coconut milk and simmer for a further 5–10 minutes until the lobster and potatoes are cooked. Serve with rice.

2 medium raw lobsters, each about 400g
2 tsp ground turmeric
1 tsp salt
150g onions, roughly chopped
4 tbsp vegetable or coconut oil
100g potatoes, peeled and cut into wedges
1 tbsp ghee* or butter
2 bay leaves
2 cloves
5cm cassia bark or cinnamon stick
2 green cardamom pods
2 tsp green chilli paste*
1½ tsp ginger-garlic paste*
1 tsp sugar
400ml coconut milk*

CARIL DE CARANGUEJOS

Goan crab curry WEST INDIA

Choosing good crabs for this recipe is critical – select those that are very fresh and feel heavy for their size, rather than the largest ones. If possible, buy live crabs and get your fishmonger to cut them up for you close to the time you want to cook. I use raw crab to ensure all the juices are retained in the sauce, but you can use blanched crab.

Cut each crab into 4 or 5 pieces (unless your fishmonger has done so for you). Make sure the small stomach sac behind the mouth and the inedible grey feathery gills are removed.

Soak the tamarind pulp in 250ml warm water for 20 minutes, then strain through a fine sieve. Mix together the ginger-garlic paste, red chilli powder, cumin and ground coriander with 3 tbsp water to make a paste.

Heat the oil in a large sauté pan and sauté the onions until softened and light brown. Add the spice paste and sauté gently for 3–4 minutes.

Add the tamarind liquid and salt. Bring to a simmer, add the crabs and simmer for about 5 minutes until almost cooked. Add the coconut milk, check the seasoning and simmer for a further 3–4 minutes until the crab is cooked. Serve with rice.

2 medium crabs (preferably raw), each about 500g
50g tamarind pulp*
2 tsp ginger-garlic paste*
1½ tsp red chilli powder
1 tsp ground cumin
½ tsp ground coriander
3 tbsp vegetable oil
150g onions, thinly sliced
½ tsp salt, or to taste
100ml coconut milk*

GARNISH:
chopped coriander leaves
crushed pepper

EGURU PETHELU

Crab with tamarind and curry leaves ANDHRA PRADESH, SOUTH INDIA

Curried crabs are a regular feature in the coastal towns of Andhra Pradesh. I first tasted this recipe in a friend's house in Kakinada – his Telangana fisherman cook made it for us. Experiencing the intense sweet flavours of seafood with simple spicing was unforgettable.

Cut each crab into 4 or 5 pieces (unless your fishmonger has done so for you) and crack the claws; set aside. Soak the tamarind pulp in 150ml warm water for 20 minutes, then strain through a fine sieve.

Heat the oil in a sauté pan, add the dried chillies and sauté for a minute or two, then remove. Add the curry leaves to the pan and sauté until they crackle. Add the onions and fry until softened and light brown.

Add the ginger-garlic paste and sauté for 3–4 minutes until it turns golden brown and the raw taste disappears. Add the coconut paste and fry for a few minutes until the oil leaves the masala. Add the ground coriander and turmeric, and sauté over a low heat for 1 minute.

Add the crabs, salt and tamarind liquid. Simmer gently for 5–8 minutes until the crab pieces are cooked, then take them out. Boil the sauce to reduce slightly. Return the crab and scatter with coriander to serve.

2 medium crabs (preferably raw), each about 500g
50g tamarind pulp*
60ml vegetable oil
2 dried red chillies
8–10 curry leaves
300g onions, thinly sliced
2 tsp ginger-garlic paste*
100g coconut paste* or creamed coconut
2 tsp ground coriander
¾ tsp ground turmeric
½ tsp salt, or to taste
2 tbsp chopped coriander leaves

POULTRY AND GAME

Chicken has a prime place in Indian cooking. I have always maintained that chickens in India taste like the real thing, unlike the majority in this country, which have been fast-bred in restrictive cages. In India, chickens exercise well and that helps to develop flavour. Before cooking poultry is skinned and cut into pieces to encourage spicy flavours to penetrate the flesh. Game is popular in India, though it is now more limited than it used to be, owing to hunting restrictions. Geese, pigeon, partridge and quail feature on luxurious Indian tables, alongside chicken and duck.

CHUTNEY NI MURGI

Chicken cooked in tangy herb paste GUJARAT, WEST INDIA

Cooking with conflicting flavours is an art, but mixing flavours, textures and colours is something that is natural to Parsi housewives. I have sampled this dish many times – my friend Chef Cyrus Todiwala cooks it to perfection.

First make the chutney. Whiz all the ingredients together in a blender with 2–3 tbsp water to make a smooth paste. Keep in the fridge until required.

Cut the chicken into 5cm cubes. Heat half the oil in a large deep sauté pan, add the onion and sauté until softened and golden. Stir in the ginger-garlic paste and sauté for 1 minute, then add the chicken. Sauté until the chicken is lightly browned, then add 120ml water, bring to the boil and simmer for 10 minutes.

Heat the rest of the oil in a separate pan, add the chutney and stir-fry until the oil separates from the chutney. Add the chicken, together with its juices, and the salt. Simmer for about 15 minutes until the chicken is cooked and the sauce has reduced to a coating consistency. Stir in the lemon juice and serve garnished with ginger and shredded mint.

500g boneless chicken thighs or breast fillets
6 tbsp sunflower oil
1 large onion, finely chopped
2 tsp ginger-garlic paste*
½ tsp salt
3 tbsp lemon juice

CHUTNEY:
100g green mango, grated
large bunch of coriander, chopped
small bunch of mint, chopped
8 garlic cloves, sliced
knob of root ginger, chopped
100g fresh coconut*, grated

GARNISH:
ginger julienne and shredded mint

CARIL DE GALINHA

Goan chicken curry GOA, WEST INDIA

As is the case in any country, every household will have its own favourite recipe for a particular dish. Chicken curry recipes are innumerable in India. Here is the Goan version – simple with straightforward bold flavours.

Joint the chicken into 8 pieces and remove the skin. Soak the tamarind pulp in 100ml warm water for 20 minutes, then strain through a fine sieve.

For the coconut spice paste, put the garlic, ginger, chillies and dry ingredients in a blender or mini-processor and process until finely ground. Add the 100ml coconut milk and whiz to a fairly smooth paste.

Heat the oil in a large deep sauté pan. Add the onions and sauté until softened and golden brown in colour. Stir in the coconut spice paste and sauté over a medium heat for 3–5 minutes.

Add the chicken pieces to the pan and sauté until they are lightly coloured. Add the salt and half the coconut milk, then simmer for about 15–20 minutes until the chicken is almost cooked. Add the tamarind liquid and remaining coconut milk. Bring to a simmer and cook for a further 5 minutes or so until the chicken is done. Sprinkle with chopped coriander and serve with boiled rice.

1.2kg whole chicken
50g tamarind pulp*
3 tbsp vegetable oil
2 onions, sliced
½ tsp salt, or to taste
400ml coconut milk*
1 tbsp coriander leaves, chopped

COCONUT SPICE PASTE:
6–8 garlic cloves, peeled
10g root ginger
4 green chillies
5 dried red chillies
1 tbsp rice flour
1 tsp coriander seeds
1 tbsp poppy seeds
1 tbsp ground turmeric
1 tsp ground cumin
100ml coconut milk*

PALOK DIYE TIKHA MURGI KALIA

Spicy chicken curry with spinach BENGAL, EAST INDIA

**This recipe reflects the merging of cooking styles. Here it is the
Muslim influence on Bengali cooking. The word *kalia* means a dark
colour sauce in Muslim Indian cooking, so this Bengali recipe has
undergone some changes in spicing and cooking technique. To me,
Calcutta has always been a great inspiration for cooking. I have
found terrific dishes with Muslim characteristics, and I dream of
returning with plenty of time on hand to explore English, Jewish and
Chinese influences on the local cuisine.**

Joint the chicken into 8 pieces and remove the skin. Heat the oil in a
deep sauté pan to smoking point, then remove from the heat and let cool
slightly. Return to a medium heat, add the dried chillies, whole spices and
bay leaf, and sauté until the spices crackle.

Add the onions and fry until softened and light brown in colour. Add the
ginger-garlic paste and cook well for 2–3 minutes to lose the raw flavour.

Add the chicken pieces and sauté to seal on all sides. Add the red chilli
powder, coriander and turmeric, and sauté for 1 minute. Stir in the chopped
tomatoes, salt and 100ml water. Bring to a simmer and cook gently for
about 20 minutes until the chicken is done.

Meanwhile, cook the spinach. Heat the oil in a separate pan and sauté
the crushed red chilli and chopped garlic for a few minutes until the garlic
turns light brown. Stir in the turmeric and salt and sauté for 30 seconds.
Add the spinach leaves and sauté until they have just wilted.

Add the wilted spinach to the chicken curry and simmer for 3–5 minutes
to allow the flavours to blend together. Remove from the heat and sprinkle
with the garam masala and chopped ginger. Serve in bowls, accompanied
by steamed rice.

1.2kg whole chicken

70ml mustard oil or vegetable oil

2 dried red chillies

3 cloves

3 black cardamom pods

2.5cm cassia bark or cinnamon stick

1 bay leaf

300g onions, sliced

10g ginger-garlic paste*

1 tsp red chilli powder

1 tsp ground coriander

1 tsp ground turmeric

250g tomatoes, chopped

½ tsp salt, or to taste

SPINACH.

30ml mustard oil

1 dried red chilli, finely crushed

1 tsp chopped garlic

½ tsp ground turmeric

½ tsp salt

500g spinach leaves, trimmed and chopped

TO SERVE:

1 tsp Bengali garam masala*

2 tsp finely chopped root ginger

HYDERABADI KALI MIRICH KA MURG

Peppery chicken curry HYDERABAD, SOUTH INDIA

Black pepper is a favoured spice in Hyderabad. This recipe brings the full flavour of freshly crushed pepper into the sauce rather than drawing on its fiery heat. The final sprinkling of toasted pepper makes a huge difference.

Joint the chicken into 8 pieces and put into a shallow dish. Mix together the ginger-garlic paste, salt, vinegar, turmeric and 1 tsp crushed pepper. Spread over the chicken, cover and marinate in the fridge for 2–3 hours.

Put the chopped large onions into a blender or food processor and process to a paste; set aside.

Heat the oil in a large deep sauté pan, add the remaining 2 tsp crushed peppercorns and sauté for 1 minute, then add the sliced onions. Cook gently until softened and golden. Next add the onion paste and fry gently for about 20 minutes until golden brown in colour.

Add the chicken with the marinade and sauté until the liquid evaporates. Add about 200ml water, bring to a simmer and cook for about 20 minutes until the chicken is done. Serve sprinkled with ginger julienne, mustard cress and toasted crushed pepper. Accompany with Indian breads.

1.2kg whole chicken
2 tsp ginger-garlic paste*
½ tsp salt, or to taste
2 tbsp white vinegar, or lemon juice
1 tsp ground turmeric
3 tsp black peppercorns, freshly crushed
2 large onions, roughly chopped
100ml vegetable oil
2 medium onions, sliced

GARNISH:
ginger julienne
mustard cress
1 tsp crushed peppercorns, lightly toasted

KOZHI VARTHA KOZHAMBU

Chettinad chicken curry TAMIL NADU, SOUTH INDIA

I must have tasted countless versions of this recipe while training as a chef in south India. I acquired this particular recipe while working in the Taj Connemara hotel from a line cook, whom we called *Thambi*, meaning younger brother. I have no idea what his real name was, but his grasp of Tamilian cooking was amazing and I learnt so many techniques from him.

Joint the chicken into 8 pieces and remove the skin. To make the spice paste, put all the ingredients in a blender or mini-processor with 3 tbsp water and whiz to a fine paste.

Heat the oil in a large deep sauté pan, add the onions and sauté until softened and light brown. Add the curry leaves and spice paste, and sauté for 2–3 minutes, then stir in the ground spices and cook, stirring, for 30 seconds.

Add the chicken pieces and sauté for a few minutes until golden. Add the coconut milk, salt and chopped tomatoes and bring to a simmer. Continue to simmer for 20 minutes or until the chicken is cooked. Sprinkle with the chopped coriander leaves to serve.

1.2kg whole chicken
70ml coconut oil or vegetable oil
200g onions, sliced
20 curry leaves
1 tsp red chilli powder
1 tsp each ground coriander and turmeric
400ml coconut milk*
½ tsp salt, or to taste
100g tomatoes, chopped
2 tbsp chopped coriander leaves

SPICE PASTE:
1 tbsp chopped root ginger
2 tbsp chopped garlic
3 cloves
10 black peppercorns
1½ tsp fennel seeds
2.5cm cassia bark or cinnamon stick

KOZHI VELLAI KAZHAMBU

White chicken curry   TAMIL NADU, SOUTH INDIA

This is one of the mild chicken curries of Tamil Nadu and I strongly recommend it – the flavours are unbelievable. Don't be put off by the lengthy ingredients list – everything is available from normal grocery stores and supermarkets. In the original recipe, shelled *mocjakka* beans are used. I have substituted broad beans, but you can omit them altogether if you prefer.

Cut the chicken into strips, about 2.5cm wide and place in a shallow dish.

To make the spice paste, heat the oil in a deep sauté pan and add the onion, ginger, garlic, spices and cashew nuts. Sauté lightly until the onions are softened, without colouring them. Allow to cool, then whiz to paste with the yogurt, using a blender or mini-processor.

Coat the chicken with the spice paste, cover and leave to marinate in a cool place for about 30 minutes.

For the seasoning, heat the oil in the clean sauté pan. Add the bay leaf and whole spices, and sauté for a minute or two. Add the onions and fry gently until they are softened and translucent.

Add the broad beans and coated chicken strips to the pan, and sauté lightly for 3–5 minutes. Add the coconut milk and ginger julienne and bring to a simmer. Continue to simmer gently for 12–15 minutes or until the chicken is cooked. Remove from the heat and add the chopped coriander leaves, lime zest and juice.

Serve the curry in bowls, garnished with coriander sprigs and lime slices. Accompany with rice.

Note: If you are able to obtain very young broad beans, use them whole in the pod, slicing diagonally into 2.5cm pieces.

500g boneless chicken breasts, skinned
70g podded broad beans
450g coconut milk*
20g ginger julienne

SPICE PASTE:
2 tsp vegetable oil
1 large onion, sliced
20g root ginger, chopped
10 garlic cloves, chopped
2.5cm cassia bark or cinnamon stick
2 cloves
2 green cardamom pods
1 tsp fennel seeds
8 green chillies
1 tsp coriander seeds
30g cashew nuts
100g yogurt

SEASONING:
2 tbsp vegetable oil
1 bay leaf
1 star anise
2 cloves
2.5cm cassia bark or cinnamon stick
2 onions, sliced

TO FINISH:
2 tbsp chopped coriander leaves
grated zest and juice of 1 lime
coriander sprigs and lime slices, to garnish

METHI KUKKUR

Chicken cooked in fenugreek leaves NORTH INDIA

Among the various greens I was forced to eat by my parents in childhood, fenugreek is something I have always enjoyed immensely. It is a versatile ingredient in Indian cooking – used as a herb, green, spice, medicine, marinade and flavour enhancer. Dried powdered fenugreek leaves give this recipe its characteristic flavour; if you are unable to obtain fresh fenugreek leaves for the garnish, simply omit. Use chicken thighs rather than joint a whole chicken if you prefer.

Joint the chicken into 8 pieces, then remove the skin and put the chicken pieces into a shallow dish. Mix the yogurt with 1 tsp salt and the green chilli paste. Spread all over the chicken, then cover and leave to marinate in a cool place for 45 minutes.

Heat the oil in a large deep sauté pan. Add the cardamom pods, cloves and cassia or cinnamon and sauté until the spices crackle. Add the sliced onions and sauté until softened and light brown in colour.

Add the ginger-garlic paste and cook well for 3–4 minutes to lose the raw aroma. Stir in the turmeric, coriander and red chilli powder and sauté for 1 minute. Add the chopped tomatoes and simmer for about 10 minutes until they are soft and the fat separates from the sauce.

Add the chicken pieces with the marinade and cook over a low heat for 15–20 minutes until the chicken is tender.

Meanwhile, prepare the garnish. Rinse the fenugreek leaves, drain well and pat dry with kitchen paper. Heat the oil for deep-frying in a deep-fryer or other deep pan to 180°C and deep-fry the fenugreek for 20–30 seconds or so until crisp. Remove with a slotted spoon as it stops crackling and drain on kitchen paper.

Add the fenugreek leaf powder, chopped ginger and coriander to the chicken, and check the seasoning. Serve topped with the deep-fried fenugreek and accompanied by Indian breads.

1.2kg whole chicken

150g yogurt

1 tsp salt, or to taste

2 tsp green chilli paste*

5 tbsp vegetable oil

6 green cardamom pods

1 black cardamom pod

3 cloves

2.5cm cassia bark or cinnamon stick

400g onions, thinly sliced

40g ginger-garlic paste*

1 tsp ground turmeric

1 tsp ground coriander

1 tsp red chilli powder

200g tomatoes, chopped

3 tsp dried fenugreek leaf powder*

1 tbsp finely chopped root ginger

2 tbsp chopped coriander leaves

GARNISH:

large handful of fresh fenugreek leaves

oil, to deep-fry

TANDOORI MURG

Tandoori spice roasted chicken NORTH INDIA

This famous dish is universally popular. Traditionally roasted in a tandoor in Indian kitchens, it is a simple recipe that can be cooked easily in a domestic oven or on the barbecue.

Joint the chicken into 4 pieces (2 legs and 2 breasts with wing bones attached). Make 3 or 4 deep incisions in each piece without cutting right through the flesh, then place in a shallow dish. Mix the lemon juice with the ginger-garlic paste, salt and chilli powder. Spread all over the chicken and set aside for 20 minutes to allow the juices to drain.

Meanwhile, mix together the ingredients for the spiced yogurt marinade. Drain the chicken, coat with the spiced yogurt mixture and set aside to marinate for 2 hours.

Preheat the oven to 200°C (180°C fan oven) mark 6. Put the chicken on a rack resting in a roasting tray and roast for 12–15 minutes. Take out of the oven and baste with the butter and oil mixture. Return the chicken to the oven and cook for a further 3–5 minutes or until it is cooked. Remove and rest on the rack for 5 minutes or so.

Serve the chicken sprinkled with lime juice and chaat masala, and accompanied by a salad and mint chutney (page 140).

1kg whole chicken
oil and melted butter, to baste
2 tbsp lemon juice
1 tbsp ginger-garlic paste*
1 tsp salt
1 tsp red chilli powder

SPICED YOGURT MARINADE:
250g thick yogurt
1 tsp garam masala
100ml vegetable oil
½ tsp ground cinnamon
½ tsp red chilli powder
1 tsp salt
pinch of edible red colouring (optional)

TO SERVE:
1½ tsp lime juice
1 tsp chaat masala*

ACHARI MURG

Rajasthani pickled chicken curry RAJASTHAN, NORTH INDIA

Rajasthan is a dry desert state and local people like to cook with a lot of oil to add succulence and preserve the food for longer. This curry has been popular in my restaurant for some time. It is a no-fuss recipe and a good meal can be built around it. The listed whole spices can be replaced with a spice mix called panch phoran* if you like.

Cut the chicken thighs in half and set aside. Heat the oil in a large deep sauté pan and add the whole spices and garlic cloves. Sauté until the spices crackle and the garlic turns light brown in colour, then add the whole red chillies and sauté for 30 seconds.

Add the sliced onions and sauté until softened and light brown in colour, then add the ginger-garlic paste and cook for 2–3 minutes. Stir in the tomato paste and 100ml water, and bring to a simmer.

Add the chicken to the pan and simmer for 15 minutes. Stir in the palm sugar if using, lemon juice and salt. Stir in the yogurt and simmer gently for a further 5 minutes; do not boil. Check the seasoning and serve sprinkled with chopped coriander leaves.

500g boneless chicken thighs, skinned
100ml vegetable oil
¼ tsp black mustard seeds
¼ tsp cumin seeds
¼ tsp fennel seeds
¼ tsp fenugreek seeds
¼ tsp onion seeds
10 peeled garlic cloves
5 red chillies
150g onions, thinly sliced
20g ginger-garlic paste*
2 tbsp tomato paste
20g palm sugar (optional)
2 tbsp lemon juice
1 tsp salt, or to taste
200g yogurt, lightly whisked
2 tbsp chopped coriander leaves

MURG TARIWALA

Home-style chicken curry   NORTH INDIA

You can't go wrong cooking this simple curry, unless you leave the pot on the stove and leave for a long vacation! It is best prepared with free-range chicken on the bone, but if you buy boneless chicken, I recommend chicken thighs.

Cut the chicken into large pieces. Pound all the whole spices together using a pestle and mortar, spice grinder or mini-processor.

Heat the oil in a saucepan. Add the spice mix and bay leaf, and sauté for a minute or two until the mixture crackles. Add the sliced onions and sauté until softened and golden brown.

Add the ginger-garlic paste, and cook gently, stirring continuously, for 2–3 minutes – keep scraping the bottom of the pan to prevent the mixture sticking and burning. Stir in the chilli powder, ground coriander and turmeric and cook briefly, stirring constantly.

Add the chopped tomatoes, tomato paste and salt. Cook over a low heat, stirring occasionally. As the tomatoes break down to form a sauce, add the chicken. Bring to a simmer and cook gently for about 20 minutes.

When the chicken is almost cooked, sprinkle with the garam masala and simmer for a little longer to finish cooking. Add the chopped coriander leaves and chopped ginger, then serve.

600g chicken thighs or breasts
6 green cardamom pods
2.5cm cassia bark or cinnamon stick
1 tsp black peppercorns
1 star anise
2 tsp cumin seeds
4 cloves
100ml vegetable oil
1 bay leaf
250g onions, finely sliced
1 tbsp ginger-garlic paste*
1½ tsp red chilli powder
1½ tsp ground coriander
1½ tsp ground turmeric
100g tomatoes, roughly chopped
1 tbsp tomato paste
1 tsp salt, or to taste
1 tsp garam masala
2 tbsp chopped coriander leaves
1 tbsp finely chopped root ginger

MURG HARA MASALA

Herb flavoured chicken   WEST INDIA

Green chicken curries are numerous in India and every region has its own. I picked up this simple, exquisite recipe from my Khoja friends in Mumbai. The Khoja Muslim community has a unique way of preparing and cooking food, which lends distinctive flavours.

Cut the chicken into 2.5cm dice. Soak the tamarind pulp in 200ml warm water for 20 minutes, then strain through a fine sieve.

To prepare the spice paste, soak the nuts in warm water to cover for 10 minutes; drain. Sauté the garlic cloves in oil until golden; cool. Put all the spice paste ingredients in a blender or mini-processor and whiz to a paste.

Heat the oil in a deep sauté pan, add the chopped ginger and green chillies and sauté for 2–3 minutes until softened. Add the spice paste and sauté lightly for a minute or two. Add the tamarind liquid and salt and bring to a simmer.

Add the chicken to the sauce and simmer for about 15–20 minutes until the chicken is cooked. Serve with rice or Indian breads.

600g boneless chicken thighs or breasts
60g tamarind pulp*
70ml vegetable oil
1 tbsp finely chopped root ginger
1½ tsp finely chopped green chillies
1 tsp salt, or to taste

SPICE PASTE:
80g cashew nuts
50g garlic cloves, peeled
oil, to fry
300g fried onion paste*
150g coriander leaves
150g mint leaves
10 green chillies
50g root ginger, roughly chopped

NAADAN KOZHI ULARTHIYATHU

Kochi chicken curry   KERALA, SOUTH INDIA

Kerala is divided geographically into three areas by its communities – north is home to the Muslims, Syrian Christians and Jews live in the centre, while the south is inhabited by Hindus. Not surprisingly, there are strong regional and cultural influences on Keralan cuisine. Every time I visit Kochi, formerly Cochin, I eat at a tiny restaurant called Naadan – literally a cooking pot. It is where I first tasted this fragrant curry, which works equally well with duck, pigeon and rabbit.

Joint the chicken into 8 pieces and remove the skin.

To make the spice powder, grind all the spices together, using a spice grinder, mini-processor or pestle and mortar.

Heat the oil in a deep sauté pan. Add the sliced onions and sauté until softened and light brown in colour. Add the ginger and garlic, and cook, stirring, for 2–3 minutes to lose the raw aromas. Add the green chillies and sauté for 1 minute. Stir in the spice powder and salt, and cook, stirring, for 30 seconds.

Pour in half of the coconut milk and 100ml water, then add the potato wedges and bring to the boil. Add the chicken pieces and simmer over a low heat for 15–20 minutes or until they are almost cooked. Add the remaining coconut milk and simmer gently until the chicken is cooked and the potatoes are tender.

In the meantime, prepare the seasoning. Heat 1 tbsp coconut oil in a separate pan and sauté the mustards seeds until they crackle. Add the sliced shallots and curry leaves, and fry gently until the shallots are softened and golden in colour.

Serve the chicken curry topped with the aromatic seasoning and accompanied by rice.

1.2kg whole chicken

SPICE POWDER:

1 star anise

3 dried red chillies

1 tbsp coriander seeds

½ tsp ground turmeric

10 black peppercorns

6 cloves

4 green cardamom pods

5cm cassia bark or cinnamon stick

TO COOK:

3 tbsp coconut oil or vegetable oil

200g onions, finely sliced

1 tbsp chopped root ginger

2 tbsp chopped garlic

4 green chillies, slit lengthways

1 tsp salt

400ml coconut milk*

150g potatoes, scrubbed and cut into wedges

SEASONING:

1 tbsp coconut oil

1 tsp black mustard seeds

50g shallots, sliced

25 curry leaves

MURG MAKHAN MASALA

Chicken in spicy tomato and onion sauce NORTH INDIA

British 'chicken tikka masala' was probably inspired by this north Indian classic. I cook tandoori chicken for this recipe to enhance the flavours, but you may use ordinary chicken or buy in ready-made tandoori chicken from your local Indian. If using raw chicken, sauté it lightly in 1 tbsp oil to seal, then cook through in the sauce.

Cut the roast chicken pieces in half, to give 8 pieces. Heat the oil in a heavy-based pan. Add the ginger and sauté for a minute, then add the tomatoes and 100ml water. Cook over a low heat for 35–40 minutes until the tomatoes break down to form a sauce. Whiz in a blender or food processor until smooth, then strain through a fine sieve and set aside.

Heat the butter in a clean pan and sauté the onion for 3 minutes until light brown in colour. Add the green chilli and tomato sauce. Bring to a simmer and add the fenugreek leaf powder, garam masala, chilli powder, honey and salt. Simmer for 30 minutes to allow the spices to blend with the sauce, then add the cream and cook for a further 3–5 minutes.

Add the chicken pieces and simmer for 10–15 minutes until the chicken is heated through. Sprinkle with chopped coriander and serve with pulao rice.

1.2kg tandoori spice roasted chicken (page 71)
2 tbsp vegetable oil
2 tbsp roughly chopped root ginger
1kg tomatoes, roughly chopped
2 tbsp butter
1 medium onion, finely sliced
1 green chilli, slit lengthways
1 tsp fenugreek leaf powder*
1 tsp garam masala
1 tsp red chilli powder
2 tbsp honey
1 tsp salt, or to taste
4 tbsp fresh single cream
2 tbsp finely chopped coriander leaves

MURGI JHOL

Bengali chicken stew BENGAL, EAST INDIA

As an east Indian by birth, I am passionate about this recipe. The first time I made it for my cousins visiting from the Punjab, they were reluctant to eat it as they considered the sauce to be very thin and the colour far too subtle – hardly a chicken curry in their view. On tasting it, they were pleasantly surprised by the flavours and delicate spicing. Now, whenever I visit them I have to cook it.

Joint the chicken into 8 pieces and remove the skin. Heat the oil in a large deep sauté pan and sauté the chicken pieces for a minute or so, without colouring. Remove from the pan and set aside.

Reheat the oil remaining in the pan. Add the panch phoran, bay leaf, cloves and cassia or cinnamon. Sauté for 1–2 minutes, then add the ginger-garlic paste and cook, stirring, for 2–3 minutes until it loses its raw taste.

Stir in the powdered spices, add the tomatoes and sauté for 2 minutes. Add the chicken and salt, cook on a low heat for 2 minutes, then add 400ml water. Bring to a simmer and add the potatoes and cauliflower. Cook for about 20 minutes until the chicken and potatoes are cooked.

Serve sprinkled with Bengali garam masala and chopped coriander.

1.2kg whole chicken
80ml vegetable oil
1 tsp panch phoran*
1 bay leaf
2 cloves
5cm cassia bark or cinnamon stick
1 tsp ginger-garlic paste*
1½ tsp ground turmeric
1 tsp ground coriander
½ tsp ground cumin
2 large tomatoes, cut into wedges
1 tsp salt, or to taste
150g potatoes, peeled and cut into wedges
150g cauliflower, cut into florets
¼ tsp Bengali garam masala*
1 tbsp coriander leaves, chopped

MASALEDAR BATYEREN

Spicy quails PUNJAB, NORTH INDIA

This recipe is a great favourite in the Punjab, my home state. Punjabi men love hunting, especially quail, and they usually take care of the preparation themselves. Obviously, they like to brag about their hunting and cooking skills ... whatever they might tell you, this dish is actually very simple to prepare.

Put the quails in a bowl, sprinkle with ½ tsp salt and coat with the yogurt. Leave to marinate for about 30 minutes.

Heat the oil in a deep sauté pan. Add the coriander seeds, cardamom pods, cloves and cassia or cinnamon, and sauté over a medium heat until they begin to crackle. Add the onions and sauté until softened and golden brown. Stir in the ginger-garlic paste and sauté for 2–3 minutes.

Add the quails and brown gently on a low heat for 3–4 minutes (without burning the onions). Add the tomatoes, remaining salt, chilli powder and ground coriander. Increase the heat and cook, stirring occasionally, for 15–20 minutes or until the fat starts to separate and the quails are cooked.

Adjust the seasoning. Sprinkle with garam masala and serve garnished with coriander. Accompany with Indian bread, such as chapattis or naan.

4 quails, skinned
1 tsp salt, or to taste
60g yogurt
4 tbsp sunflower oil
1 tbsp coriander seeds
10 green cardamom pods
5 cloves
2 x 2.5cm cassia bark or cinnamon sticks
200g onions, thinly sliced
2 tbsp ginger-garlic paste*
6 tomatoes, diced
2 tsp red chilli powder
2 tsp ground coriander
1 tsp garam masala
handful of coriander sprigs, to garnish

SURTI SANTARA NA CHHAL MA BATHAK

Duck curry with orange GUJARAT, WEST INDIA

Gujarat may be a dry state, but it has a cuisine that is varied and full of flavours. In this unusual Parsi-influenced recipe, the calming orange flavour works well with the exotic warm spice blends.

Cut each duck breast into 4 or 5 pieces. Heat the oil in a large deep sauté pan, add the whole spices and sauté until they begin to crackle. Add the sliced onions and sauté until softened and light brown in colour.

Add the ginger-garlic paste and chillies; cook, stirring, for 2–3 minutes. Add the chilli powder, turmeric and cumin, and sauté for 30 seconds.

Add the duck pieces to the pan and sauté until light brown in colour all over. Stir in the tomatoes and ½ tsp salt, then add 100ml water and half of the orange juice. Bring to a simmer and cook gently for 20 minutes or until the duck is almost cooked.

In the meantime, cut the orange zest into julienne strips and blanch in boiling water for 1 minute, then drain and set aside.

Add the orange zest julienne and remaining orange juice to the pan and simmer until the duck is cooked. Check the seasoning and sprinkle with chopped coriander and garam masala to serve.

600g skinless duck breast fillets
100ml vegetable oil
½ tsp cumin seeds
5cm cassia bark or cinnamon stick
2 cloves
4 green cardamom pods
200g onions, sliced
2 tsp ginger-garlic paste*
3 green chillies, chopped
1 tsp red chilli powder
1 tsp ground turmeric
2 tsp ground cumin
100g tomatoes, chopped
½ tsp salt, or to taste
300ml orange juice
finely pared zest of 1 orange
1 tbsp coriander leaves, chopped
½ tsp garam masala

PURA KICHILI PAZHAM MELAGU KARI

Pigeon cooked with Chettinad spices TAMIL NADU, SOUTH INDIA

Pigeon is not a common game bird in Indian cuisine, but there are some interesting, unusual recipes to be found within lesser-known communities. Chettiars, for example, have always been big on game. Wild boar, pigeon, hare and deer are among their favourites. For this recipe, you need to use wild pigeon with its highly flavoured, dense flesh, rather than the milder farmed alternative; the younger the pigeon, the better the flavour and texture. Do include the liver – it enhances the flavour of the dish.

Joint each pigeon into 4 pieces (2 legs and 2 breasts with wing bones attached) and remove the skin. Put the pigeon pieces in a shallow dish. Mix together the orange juice, ginger-garlic paste, turmeric and salt, then spoon over the pigeon pieces and turn to coat all over. Set aside to marinate in a cool place for at least 30 minutes. (Reserve the orange zest for the garnish.)

In the meantime, prepare the toasted spice powder. Dry-fry the spices in a heavy-based frying pan over a medium heat for 2–3 minutes until they crackle, shaking the pan constantly. Allow to cool, then grind to a powder, using a spice grinder, pestle and mortar or mini-processor. Set aside.

When ready to cook, heat the oil in a pan, add the curry leaves and sauté for a minute or two, then add the sliced onions and fry until softened and golden brown in colour.

Add the toasted spice powder, sauté for a minute, then add the pigeon (including the liver) together with the marinade. Sauté for a few minutes until the pigeon pieces are lightly browned. Add 250ml water and bring to a simmer. Cook slowly for about 45 minutes until the pigeon is tender.

Add the chopped coriander leaves and grated orange zest. Stir well and serve hot, with chapattis.

2 wood pigeons, cleaned (liver reserved)
grated zest and juice of 1 orange
2 tsp ginger-garlic paste*
½ tsp ground turmeric
1 tsp salt

TOASTED SPICE POWDER:
1 tsp black peppercorns
1 tsp cumin seeds
2 tsp fennel seeds
1 star anise
5 green cardamom pods
2 cloves
2.5cm cassia bark or cinnamon stick

TO COOK:
4 tbsp vegetable oil
10 curry leaves
2 medium onions, thinly sliced
4 tbsp chopped coriander leaves

LAGAN KA TITAR

Slow-cooked partridge   NORTH INDIA

Until recently in India, *chidimaar* – or bird hunters – were very common. Most game birds were bought from these hunters, who would sell their merchandise from door to door. Since the Indian government has imposed certain restrictions on killing game, the profession has declined. This recipe is named after the dish it is traditionally cooked in – a *lagan* is a casserole with a tight-fitting lid, for slow cooking on charcoal. A well-sealed casserole in a domestic oven is just as effective. Marinating game birds prior to slow cooking helps to make them succulent and juicy.

Joint the partridges into 4 pieces (2 legs and 2 breasts with wing bones attached) and remove the skin. Place in a shallow dish, spread with the ginger-garlic paste and sprinkle with the salt. Set aside for 30 minutes.

Meanwhile, to make the spice powder, grind the spices together to a fine powder, using a spice grinder, pestle and mortar or mini-processor. Set aside.

For the seeded coconut paste, toast the poppy seeds, coconut and nuts or melon seeds together in a dry frying pan over a medium heat until golden. Cool slightly, then put into a blender or mini-processor with 2 tbsp water and whiz to a fine paste.

Mix the spice paste, seeded coconut paste, yogurt and fried onion paste together in a large casserole with a tight-fitting lid. Stir in the remaining ingredients with 800ml water. Add the partridge pieces, turn to coat, cover and set aside to marinate for 30 minutes. Meanwhile, preheat the oven to 170°C (150°C fan oven) mark 3.

Mix a cupful of flour with enough water to make a paste and spread around the rim of the casserole to seal the lid. Put the casserole in the oven and cook for 35–45 minutes or until the partridge is tender. Serve sprinkled with chopped coriander leaves.

2 partridges, cleaned
1½ tbsp ginger-garlic paste*
1 tsp salt

SPICE POWDER:
1 tsp black peppercorns
1 black cardamom pod
6 green cardamom pods
2.5cm cassia bark or cinnamon stick
1 mace blade
¼ tsp freshly grated nutmeg

SEEDED COCONUT PASTE:
10g white poppy seeds
30g unsweetened desiccated coconut*, toasted
20g chironji nuts or melon seeds, toasted

TO MARINATE:
200g thick yogurt
100g fried onion paste*
100g butter, melted
3–5 cloves
1 bay leaf
10g almond slivers
10g pistachio slivers
5–6 saffron threads, infused in 1 tbsp milk
1 tbsp kewra water (screwpine flower essence)*

GARNISH:
1 tbsp chopped coriander leaves

MEAT

Prior to Muslim invasions, the British Raj and other foreign influences, meat was eaten by the warrior clans only, as the rest of the Indian community was purely vegetarian. These days, more people eat meat. Lamb is popular in Kashmir, but elsewhere goat is the predominant meat, as beef and pork are rarely eaten. Venison only features on restaurant menus and lavish tables. Indians eat their meat well cooked – just cooked or underdone is not a concept in Indian cooking. As you travel from region to region, you find fascinating differences in cooking techniques, especially with spicing.

ROGAN JOSH

Kashmiri lamb curry   KASHMIR, NORTH INDIA

Rogan josh is a classical preparation, traditionally made with lamb, and only lamb. There are various claims to the origin of the name. Some claim that the violet bark of a Kashmiri tree called *ratanjog* **should be boiled in oil to prepare** *rogan* **and this oil is used to make the curry. Others say** *rogan* **simply describes red coloured chilli oil that floats on the surface of the dish. Recently, I met up with some old school friends from Kashmiri who informed me that** *marwal ka phool* **(cock's comb flower extract) should be used to give** *rogan josh* **its characteristic colour. To keep it simple, I use the colour from red chillies and tomato paste to give the right appearance. The inclusion of almonds is another source of controversy. I marinate the lamb in a mixture of crushed almonds, saffron and yogurt to create a canvas for the spectrum of spice flavours that follows during the cooking. It also makes sense to use local ingredients indigenous to Kashmir for a classic recipe of the state.**

Put the lamb into a shallow dish. For the marinade, whisk the yogurt with the saffron and almonds. Add to the lamb, turn to coat and set aside to marinate in a cool place for 2 hours.

To prepare the garam masala, pound the spices together to a powder, using a spice grinder, pestle and mortar or mini-processor.

Heat the oil in a heavy-based pan, add the pounded garam masala and stir until the spices begin to crackle. Add the sliced onions, stir and cook for 8–12 minutes until softened and golden brown. Add the ginger-garlic paste and sauté for 2–3 minutes.

Add the lamb, together with the marinade, stir and cook for about 30 minutes until the meat is browned and three-quarters cooked. (The lamb will cook in its own juices, but if there is very little liquid in the pan, some water or lamb stock can be added. Once the meat is browned, it will tend to stick to the bottom of the pan, so keep stirring and scraping the bottom – this is important to develop the characteristic flavour.)

Add the powdered spices and cook for 3–5 minutes, adding a little water if required. Stir in the salt and tomato paste and cook, stirring, until the lamb is tender. Finally, stir in the chopped coriander.

Serve garnished with red chillies, and accompanied by coriander chutney and saffron rice or an Indian bread.

1kg leg of lamb, cut into 5cm pieces on the bone

MARINADE:
150g yogurt, lightly whisked
pinch of saffron threads
2 tbsp crushed blanched almonds

GARAM MASALA:
1½ tsp cumin seeds
6 green cardamom pods
2 black cardamom pods
2.5cm cassia bark or cinnamon stick
8 cloves
2 mace blades
1 tbsp black peppercorns

TO COOK:
6 tbsp vegetable oil
350g onions, finely sliced
2 tbsp ginger-garlic paste*
1½ tsp red chilli powder
2 tbsp ground coriander
1 tsp garam masala
1 tsp ground turmeric
½ tsp salt, or to taste
2 tbsp tomato paste
3 tbsp finely chopped coriander leaves

TO SERVE:
dried red chillies
coriander chutney (page 138)

VADAMA KARI KOZHAMBU

Almond lamb curry   TAMIL NADU, SOUTH INDIA

Traditionally, this preparation takes its flavour from *vadagam* – a powdered, sun-dried blend of lentils and spices, which is tedious to make at home. Some Asian grocers stock it, but for this recipe I have simplified the flavours and used whole spices – it works well.

Cut the lamb into 4cm pieces. Soak the almonds in warm water to cover for 10 minutes, then drain and blend to a paste with the poppy seeds, using a blender or mini-processor. Soak the tamarind pulp in 4 tbsp warm water for 20 minutes, then strain through a fine sieve.

Heat the oil in a deep sauté pan, add the whole spices and curry leaves, and sauté until the spices crackle. Add the chopped onions and fry until softened and golden brown in colour. Add the ginger-garlic paste and cook, stirring, for 2–3 minutes to lose the raw taste.

Add the tomatoes and cook for about 10 minutes. Stir in the powdered spices and cook, stirring, for 2–3 minutes, adding a little water if needed.

Add the lamb and sauté to seal on all sides. Add salt and 200ml water. Cook on a low heat for 30 minutes. Stir in the almond paste and tamarind liquid, and simmer for 15 minutes or until the lamb is cooked, adding a little water if the sauce is too thick. Serve sprinkled with almonds and coriander.

500g boneless leg of lamb
200g blanched almonds
2 tsp poppy seeds
30g tamarind pulp*
2 tbsp oil
3 cloves
2 cinnamon sticks
3 green cardamom pods
8 curry leaves
2 medium onions, chopped
2 tsp ginger-garlic paste*
2 medium tomatoes, chopped
½ tsp ground turmeric
3 tsp ground coriander
2 tsp red chilli powder
1 tsp salt, or to taste
20 almond slivers, lightly toasted
coriander sprigs, to garnish

GHAZAALA

Lamb with green chillies   HYDERABAD, SOUTH INDIA

Most of the heat in chillies comes from the seeds and white membrane – remove these and you will reduce the heat by about 80%, yet still provide a great flavour kick. Fat chillies are less fiery but flavourful – essential for recipes calling for green chilli flavour rather than heat.

Cut the lamb into 2.5cm cubes. Whiz half the chillies in a blender to a paste, then tip into a bowl and mix with the yogurt, turmeric, crushed coriander and salt. Cover and set aside.

Heat the oil in a deep sauté pan and sauté the remaining chillies for 2 minutes; remove and keep aside. Sauté the sliced onions in the oil remaining in the pan until softened and light brown in colour.

Add the lamb and sauté until browned on all sides. Cook gently, stirring frequently, for 15–20 minutes to evaporate all the juices. Add the ginger-garlic paste and sauté well for 2–3 minutes to lose the raw taste.

Add the yogurt mixture with 200ml water and simmer for 20 minutes or until the lamb is cooked. Add the fried chillies and chopped coriander and simmer for a few minutes. Add the lime zest and juice, then serve with rice.

500g boneless leg of lamb
100g fat green chillies, slit lengthways
  and deseeded
200g yogurt
1 tsp ground turmeric
3 tsp coriander seeds, toasted and
  roughly crushed
1 tsp salt, or to taste
60ml vegetable oil
600g onions, thinly sliced
2 tsp ginger-garlic paste*
4 tbsp chopped coriander leaves
grated zest and juice of 3 limes

SALLI MA KHARU GOSHT

Parsi lamb curry with straw potatoes WEST INDIA

This has been a favourite Parsi dish in Indian restaurants for a long time. It's a great recipe, without a great deal of ingredients, and cooks well. The presentation is dramatic, but adds to the appeal.

Cut the lamb into 4cm cubes. Heat the oil in a deep sauté pan and sauté the whole spices and dried red chilli until they crackle. Add the sliced onions and fry until softened and golden brown in colour.

Add 3 tbsp water and simmer until the water evaporates, then add the ginger-garlic paste and sauté for 2 minutes to lose the raw taste. Add the turmeric, cumin, chilli powder and salt, and cook, stirring, for 1 minute.

Add the lamb, together with the chopped tomatoes if using, and sauté for 3–5 minutes until well browned.

Add the green chillies and 100ml water and bring to a simmer. Cook over a low heat, stirring frequently, for 40 minutes until the lamb is cooked.

Meanwhile, for the garnish, peel the potatoes and cut into fine strips; pat dry on kitchen paper. Heat the oil for deep-frying in a suitable pan to 190°C and deep-fry the potatoes in small batches for 2–3 minutes until crisp and golden. Remove with a slotted spoon and drain on kitchen paper.

Spoon the curry into bowls and sprinkle with the shredded coriander. Pile the fried julienne potatoes on top and serve.

500g boneless leg of lamb
4 tbsp vegetable oil
2.5cm cassia bark or cinnamon stick
2 cloves
3 green cardamom pods
1 dried red chilli
3 large onions, sliced
1½ tsp ginger-garlic paste*
1 tsp ground turmeric
2 tsp ground cumin
1 tsp red chilli powder
1 tsp salt
2 tomatoes, chopped (optional)
3 green chillies, slit lengthways
    and deseeded

GARNISH:
2 potatoes
vegetable oil, to deep-fry
shredded coriander leaves

KOSHA MANGSHO

Dry lamb curry WEST BENGAL, EAST INDIA

This easy curry will satisfy a craving for spicy thick gravy with lots of meat essence. *Sukha gosht* and *bhuna gosht* are similar dry, spicy preparations but this recipe has its regional characteristics. It is perfect with thin chapattis, or you could serve it with tortilla bread.

Put the lamb into a shallow dish. Mix the yogurt with the salt and turmeric, add to the lamb, and turn to coat all over. Set aside to marinate in a cool place for 45 minutes.

Heat the oil in a deep sauté pan, add the onions and sauté until softened and lightly coloured. Add the lamb with the marinade and sauté to seal and brown on all sides.

Add the ginger-garlic paste and sauté for 2–3 minutes to lose the raw taste, then add the powdered spices and sauté for a minute. Stir in the tomato paste and 300ml water. Bring to a simmer and cook on a low heat for about 40 minutes until the lamb is cooked.

Serve hot, sprinkled with garam masala and chopped coriander.

1kg leg of lamb, cut into 5cm pieces
    on the bone
100g yogurt
1 tsp salt, or to taste
1 tsp ground turmeric
6 tbsp vegetable oil
150g onions, sliced
3 tsp ginger-garlic paste*
2½ tsp ground coriander
2 tsp ground cumin
1½ tsp red chilli powder
1 tbsp tomato paste, or 2 chopped tomatoes
½ tsp Bengali garam masala*
1 tbsp coriander leaves, chopped

CHAAP KARI VARUVAL

Lamb chop curry   TAMIL NADU, SOUTH INDIA

This recipe belongs to a region where I would like be born again. The cuisine is so intricate that it is said you must be born Chettiar to be able to cook the food properly. Nattulkotai Chettiars were a nomadic trading community that once roamed and sailed through south India and south-east Asian countries assimilating local foods, such as sticky red rice, into their own cuisine. Their unusual spices are *kalpasi*, a stone fungus, and *marathi mukka*, buds from a local tree akin to cloves. These give characteristic flavour to Chettinad dishes, but they are not available here, so I have developed a similar flavour profile using simple spices.

Flatten the lamb chops with a wooden mallet and place in a shallow dish. Combine the yogurt, turmeric and salt. Coat the lamb chops with the spiced yogurt and set aside in a cool place to marinate for 1 hour.

To make the spice paste, heat the 1 tbsp oil in a frying pan, add the whole spices and sauté until they crackle. Add the sliced onion and sauté until softened and golden brown. Add the ginger-garlic paste and cook for a few minutes to lose the raw aroma. Add the tomatoes and green chillies and cook until the fat separates from the mixture. Stir in the chopped coriander and set aside for 5 minutes to cool slightly. Transfer to a blender and process to a fine paste. Tip into a bowl and set aside.

For the seasoning, heat the oil in a deep sauté pan and sauté the bay leaves, cassia or cinnamon, cardamom pod and clove for 1 minute. Add the sliced onions and cook until translucent. Add the spice paste and sauté until golden in colour.

Add the lamb chops and continue cooking until the oil begins to separate from the spice paste. Add the lime juice, check the seasoning and continue to cook until the chops are tender.

Arrange the chops in a warmed serving dish and garnish with chopped coriander leaves and ginger julienne to serve.

300g French-trimmed lamb cutlets

2 tbsp yogurt

1 tsp ground turmeric

1 tsp salt, or to taste

1 tbsp lime juice

SPICE PASTE:

1 tbsp oil

2 tsp coriander seeds

1 tsp black peppercorns

1 tsp fennel seeds

3 cloves

2.5cm cassia bark or cinnamon stick

2 green cardamom pods

1 medium onion, finely sliced

1 tbsp ginger-garlic paste*

2 tomatoes, roughly chopped

4 green chillies, finely chopped

4 tbsp coriander leaves, finely chopped

SEASONING:

2½ tbsp oil

2 bay leaves

2.5cm cassia bark or cinnamon stick

1 green cardamom pod

1 clove

2 medium onions, sliced

GARNISH:

chopped coriander leaves

ginger julienne

RAAN E SIKANDER

Spiced roast leg of lamb NORTH INDIA

This is a traditional recipe with Afghan influence. The combination of braising and roasting makes the lamb really succulent and juicy.

Make a few deep cuts in the surface of the lamb. Mix the ginger-garlic paste with 1½ tsp chilli powder and 3 tbsp oil, and massage over the lamb and into the cuts. Marinate at room temperature for 2 hours, then in the fridge for another 2 hours. Preheat oven to 170°C (150°C fan oven) mark 3.

Heat the remaining oil in a large flameproof casserole (which can hold the lamb). Add the whole spices and bay leaf. Sauté for 1 minute, then add the onions and cook until softened. Stir in the remaining 1 tsp chilli powder and other ground spices and sauté until the oil leaves the masala.

Stir in the tomato paste and salt, then add the leg of lamb. Seal the pan with foil and a lid and cook in the oven for 50 minutes to 1½ hours until the lamb is very tender, turning it once or twice during cooking.

Take out the lamb and put under a hot grill for a few minutes, turning to lightly char the surface. Meanwhile, let the sauce bubble on the hob to reduce and thicken, then strain. Carve the lamb and serve with the sauce.

1 small leg of lamb, about 1kg, trimmed
4 tbsp ginger-garlic paste*
2½ tsp red chilli powder
120ml vegetable oil
3 cloves
4 green cardamom pods
3 black cardamom pods
5cm cassia bark or cinnamon stick
2 star anise
1 bay leaf
4 medium onions, finely sliced
2 tsp ground coriander
2 tsp ground cumin
1 tsp ground turmeric
1 tbsp tomato paste
1 tsp salt, or to taste

KAIRI KA GOSHT DO PIAZA

Lamb in mango and onion sauce SOUTH INDIA

Do-piaza implies the addition of onions to a dish twice. Lucknow and Hyderabad both claim the authentic version; I have chosen the Hyderabadi version because of the interesting inclusion of mango.

Cut the lamb into 2.5cm cubes. Whiz half of the onions in a blender or food processor to make a smooth paste. Slice the remaining onions.

Heat the oil in a deep sauté pan and fry the sliced onions until softened and golden brown; remove and set aside. Add the onion paste and sauté for 3–5 minutes until golden brown. Stir in the ginger-garlic paste and cook well for 2–3 minutes. Add the powdered spices and sauté for 30 seconds.

Add the lamb and salt, and cook, stirring, for 3–5 minutes until lightly browned. Add 100ml water and simmer for a few minutes, then add the mango, sugar and chillies. Cook gently for 30 minutes or until the lamb is almost tender, adding a little more water if needed.

Meanwhile, whiz the coriander leaves to a paste in a blender. Stir into the sauce with the curry leaves and simmer for a further 10 minutes.

For the seasoning, heat the 1 tbsp oil in another pan and fry the mustard seeds, chillies and garlic until lightly browned. Pour over the do-piaza, cover and serve immediately to retain the flavours. Serve with Indian bread.

600g boneless leg of lamb
4 medium onions
5 tbsp vegetable oil
1 tbsp ginger-garlic paste*
½ tsp ground turmeric
1 tsp garam masala
1 tsp red chilli powder
1 tsp salt, or to taste
1 mango, peeled and cut into julienne
1 tsp sugar
3 green chillies, finely chopped
60g coriander leaves
10 curry leaves, roughly chopped

SEASONING:
1 tbsp oil
1 tsp black mustard seeds
2 green chillies, slit lengthways
4 garlic cloves, sliced

MARATHI NALLI GOSHT

Marathi-style lamb shank   SHOLAPUR, WEST INDIA

The textures and flavours are wonderfully varied in this region and the spicing is quite unique. Peanuts, sesame seeds, red chillies, onions and garlic are some of the common flavourings. This recipe belongs to the Maratha warriors, as they were the privileged clan who were allowed to eat meat.

Put the lamb shanks into a shallow dish. Mix together the ingredients for the marinade and apply to the lamb shanks, massaging well. Cover and leave to marinate in the fridge for 4–6 hours.

To prepare the roasted spice blend, dry-fry the dried chillies, spices and sesame seeds in a heavy-based frying pan over a medium heat for 2–3 minutes until they crackle, shaking the pan constantly. Allow to cool, then grind to a powder, using a spice grinder, pestle and mortar or mini-processor; set aside.

For the sauce, thinly slice two of the onions; finely chop the other one and set aside. Heat the oil in a flameproof casserole or heavy-based deep pan. Add the sliced onions and fry until softened and golden. Add the chopped onion and sauté until softened and brown in colour, then add the ginger-garlic paste and sauté for 2–3 minutes to lose the raw taste. Stir in the turmeric and roasted spice blend and sauté for 30 seconds.

Add the lamb shanks to the casserole or pan and sauté to seal all over, then add the tomato paste, salt and 100ml water, and bring to a simmer, stirring. Cover and cook over a low heat or transfer to a preheated oven at 180°C (160°C fan oven) mark 4 and cook for about 45 minutes until the lamb shanks are tender. Uncover for the final 10 minutes' cooking.

Remove the lamb shanks from the sauce and place on a warmed platter; keep warm. Whiz the sauce in a blender until smooth, then pass through a sieve into a clean pan and reheat gently. Finally, stir in the chopped coriander.

Serve the lamb shanks with the sauce poured over and garnished with shredded spring onion.

2 lamb shanks

MARINADE:

1 tsp crushed dried red chilli

1 tbsp ginger-garlic paste*

½ tsp ground turmeric

3 tbsp yogurt

1 tbsp lime juice

2 tbsp vegetable oil

ROASTED SPICE BLEND:

4 dried red chillies

5cm cassia bark or cinnamon stick

8 cloves

8 green cardamom pods

2 black cardamom pods

2 tbsp coriander seeds

1 tsp sesame seeds

SAUCE:

3 large onions

5 tbsp vegetable oil

1½ tbsp ginger-garlic paste*

1½ tsp ground turmeric

1 tbsp tomato paste

½ tsp salt, or to taste

1 tbsp chopped coriander leaves

GARNISH:

shredded spring onion

MANGSHO GHUGNI

Lamb curry with chickpeas BENGAL, EAST INDIA

Mangsho is meat and generally meat for the people of Hindu Bengali origin is *panther*, which is goat meat. This traditional curry is normally made with diced meat, though here I have used lamb steaks. I like to cook the chickpeas, but you can use canned ones.

Drain the chickpeas, put into a saucepan and cover with fresh water. Add 1 bay leaf, 1 clove and 1 cardamom pod and bring to the boil. Lower the heat and simmer until the chickpeas are cooked, about 2 hours. Season with ½ tsp salt towards the end of cooking. Drain and set aside.

Heat the oil in a deep sauté pan. Add the remaining bay leaves, cloves, and cardamom pods and sauté until they crackle. Add the onions and sauté until softened and translucent. Add the ginger-garlic paste and cook, stirring, for 2–3 minutes. Add the ground coriander, chilli powder and cumin and stir for 30 seconds.

Add the tomatoes, lamb steaks, salt and just enough water to cover the mixture. Cook gently for about 30 minutes. Add the chickpeas and simmer for a further 5–10 minutes or until the lamb is cooked. Serve sprinkled with garam masala. Garnish with chopped coriander and ginger julienne.

150g chickpeas, soaked in cold water overnight
3 bay leaves
7 cloves
4 black cardamom pods
1 tsp salt, or to taste
6 tbsp vegetable oil or mustard oil
200g onions, finely sliced
1½ tbsp ginger-garlic paste*
1 tsp ground coriander
1 tsp red chilli powder
1 tsp ground cumin
200g tomatoes, finely chopped
4 lamb leg steaks, each about 100g

GARNISH:
½ tsp Bengali garam masala*
chopped coriander leaves
ginger julienne

ALOO GOSHT SALAN

Lamb with potatoes BIHAR, EAST INDIA

Cooking lamb with potatoes is very common in eastern India. This tempting recipe is almost like a spicy stew – the potatoes absorb the lamb juices to delicious effect.

Cut the lamb into 4cm cubes. Heat the oil in a deep heavy-based sauté pan and add the chopped ginger. Sauté for 30 seconds, then add the bay leaves, cloves, cardamom pods and cumin seeds, and sauté well until the spices crackle. Add the onions and fry until softened and golden brown.

Add the lamb and sauté well for 10–12 minutes to seal and brown on all sides. Stir in the chilli powder, ground coriander and turmeric. Add the potato wedges and sauté for 2–3 minutes. Add 200ml water and the salt. Bring to a simmer and cook gently for 15 minutes or until the potatoes are nearly tender.

Meanwhile, cut the spring onions into 2.5cm lengths and the red pepper into wide strips. Add to the pan with the tomatoes and cook for a further 5–10 minutes until the lamb is tender.

Serve sprinkled with garam masala and chopped coriander. Accompany with boiled rice or an Indian bread.

600g boneless leg of lamb
4 tbsp vegetable oil
2 tbsp finely chopped root ginger
2 bay leaves
4 cloves
2 black cardamom pods
1½ tsp cumin seeds
4 medium onions, finely sliced
1 tsp red chilli powder
1½ tsp ground coriander
1½ tsp ground turmeric
2 medium potatoes, scrubbed and cut into wedges
½ tsp salt, or to taste
4 spring onions, trimmed
1 red pepper, cored and deseeded
3 medium tomatoes, cut into wedges
½ tsp garam masala
1 tbsp chopped coriander leaves

ERACHI OLARTHIYATHU

Syrian Christian lamb curry KERALA, SOUTH INDIA

At my chef school I was really impressed with Chef George K George who was one year my senior. I caught up with George in Kochi in 2002. He had not changed a bit since college days – same cool, easy attitude, a very contented soul. George has been a great influence on my learning of Keralan food. He is a dedicated Syrian Christian and a true chef. I have tried to recreate his beef curry as a lamb curry – it's a great recipe ... by George!

Cut the lamb into 2.5cm cubes. Put the ingredients for the spice paste in a blender or mini-processor and grind to a fine paste.

Put the lamb into a heavy-based pan with the spice paste, sliced onion, garlic, ginger julienne, curry leaves, coconut slices, salt and 3–4 tbsp water. Bring to a simmer and cook gently for 35–40 minutes, stirring frequently, until the meat is tender.

For the final spicing, heat the oil in a separate pan and sauté the onions with the curry leaves until the onions are softened and brown in colour. Add this spicing to the meat and cook slowly for a further 5–7 minutes. Serve garnished with chopped coriander leaves.

500g boneless leg of lamb

SPICE PASTE:

1 tsp red chilli powder

2 tsp ground coriander

$\frac{1}{2}$ tsp ground turmeric

$\frac{1}{2}$ tsp cumin seeds

$\frac{1}{2}$ tsp black peppercorns

2 star anise

2.5cm cassia bark or cinnamon stick

2 cloves

2 green cardamom pods

50ml white vinegar

TO COOK:

1 medium onion, sliced

2 garlic cloves, sliced

10g root ginger julienne

10 curry leaves

50g fresh coconut*, thinly sliced

1 tsp salt, or to taste

FINAL SPICING:

4 tbsp vegetable oil

2 medium onions, thinly sliced

10 curry leaves

GARNISH:

2 tbsp chopped coriander leaves

MAMSA ISHTEW

Aromatic stew with coconut milk KARNATAKA, SOUTH INDIA

This beautiful lamb stew is a speciality of Mangalore and the Karvari coast – a very colourful part of Karnataka with a wide spectrum of flavours. The community in Mangalore is predominantly Catholic and prepares some of the hottest and the mildest food of India. The list of ingredients can be a little intimidating, but the result is spectacular and you'll probably find you have most of the spices already. Almost every south Indian state will have its own version of lamb stew – this is one of my favourites.

Cut the lamb into 4cm cubes and place in a deep heavy-based pan with the coconut milk, three-quarters of the ginger julienne, the lemon juice and salt. Simmer for about 30 minutes until the lamb is three-quarters cooked.

Meanwhile, heat the oil in a separate pan and sauté the garlic gently for a minute without colouring. Add the curry leaves, whole spices and bay leaves, and sauté until the spices crackle.

Add the sliced onions and green chillies and fry gently until the onion is softened, but not coloured. Add the peppercorns, turmeric, cumin and ground fennel seeds and sauté for 30 seconds or so. Add the potatoes and sauté for 8–10 minutes until sealed and golden brown on all sides.

Add the spice mixture to the lamb and stir well. Cook on a low heat for a further 15–20 minutes until the lamb is very tender. Garnish with the remaining ginger julienne to serve.

500g boneless leg of lamb

400ml coconut milk*

10g root ginger julienne

2 tsp lemon juice

1 tsp salt, or to taste

3 tbsp vegetable oil

6 garlic cloves, sliced

10 curry leaves

1 star anise

5cm cassia bark or cinnamon stick

8 cloves

5 green cardamom pods

2 bay leaves

2 medium onions, thinly sliced

2 green chillies, slit lengthways

1/2 tsp black peppercorns

1 tsp ground turmeric

2 tsp ground cumin

2 tsp ground fennel seeds

4 small Jersey Royal potatoes, scrubbed and halved

LAAL MAAS

Rajasthani red lamb curry RAJASTHAN, NORTH INDIA

This curry is prepared with red chilli paste and the authentic dish is very hot – even hotter than 'British vindaloo'. I have adjusted the recipe to suit most palates. In India, goat meat would normally feature where I have used lamb in my recipes. For this curry, you could use any meat.

Trim the lamb if necessary. Whisk together the yogurt, crushed dried chillies and cumin seeds, ground spices and salt in a bowl; set aside.

Heat the oil in a deep sauté pan and sauté the garlic until light brown in colour. Add all the cardamom pods and sauté until they crackle. Add the sliced onions and fry, stirring, until softened and light brown in colour.

Add the lamb and sauté over a medium heat to seal and lightly colour. Add the tomato paste and stir over a low heat for 10 minutes.

Add the spiced yogurt, stir and cook over a low heat for 30–40 minutes or until the lamb is tender. Adjust the seasoning. Finally, stir in the chopped coriander leaves.

Serve topped with a quenelle of spiced raita.

Spiced raita: Mix 50g Greek yogurt with 1 tsp chopped coriander leaves, ¼ tsp toasted cumin seeds and a pinch of crushed dried red chilli.

1kg leg of lamb, cut into 5cm pieces
   on the bone
250g yogurt
10 dried red chillies, crushed
1 tsp cumin seeds, toasted and lightly crushed
3 tsp ground coriander
1 tsp ground turmeric
1 tsp garam masala
1 tsp salt
5 tbsp vegetable oil
12 garlic cloves, sliced
5 black cardamom pods
5 green cardamom pods
3 medium onions, finely sliced
2 tbsp tomato paste
2 tbsp chopped coriander leaves
spiced raita (see left), to serve

KHEEMA MATTAR

Ground lamb with peas and cumin NORTH INDIA

Indians are very fond of cooking minced meat with vegetables. I particularly like lamb mince cooked with green peas or potatoes, and this is the recipe I serve in my restaurant. Of course, you could vary the vegetable; simply cut it into small pieces.

Put the meat to one side. Heat the oil in a deep sauté pan and sauté the whole spices, bay leaf and crushed black pepper until they crackle. Add the chopped onions and sauté until softened and light brown in colour.

Add the ginger-garlic paste and cook well for 2–3 minutes, then add the green chillies, lamb mince and salt. Cook, stirring, for 3–5 minutes until the meat is evenly coloured.

Add the tomato paste and 250ml water, and bring to a simmer. Cook gently for 15–20 minutes until the lamb is cooked. Add the peas and cook for a further 5–10 minutes until they are tender.

Serve sprinkled with the garam masala and chopped coriander leaves. Accompany with chapattis or any other Indian bread.

500g boneless leg of lamb, finely minced
6 tbsp vegetable oil
3 cloves
2 green cardamom pods
2.5cm cassia bark or cinnamon stick
1 bay leaf
1 tsp crushed black pepper
2 medium onions, finely chopped
2 tsp ginger-garlic paste*
5 green chillies, slit lengthways
1 tsp salt
3 tbsp tomato paste
150g shelled green peas
½ tsp garam masala
2 tbsp chopped coriander leaves

GOSHT KI BIRYANI

Lamb cooked with rice NORTH INDIA

There are communities in India that specialise in cooking biryani and practise it professionally. In Matka Peer in New Delhi, for example, people leave their cooking pots with chefs in the morning and collect their biryani in the evening – after it has cooked slowly on charcoal ashes for 3–4 hours. Lucknow and Hyderabad are particularly renowned for biryani cooking.

Of the various methods of cooking this dish, I have given a simple one that ensures the rice and lamb are both cooked properly. It can be served as a meal in itself, with a simple raita.

Cut the lamb into 2.5cm cubes and place in a shallow dish. For the marinade, deep-fry the onions in the hot oil until crisp and brown, drain on kitchen paper and cool. Put the cooled onions in a blender and whiz to a paste, then add the yogurt with the rest of the marinade ingredients and process briefly until smooth. Coat the lamb with the mixture and leave to marinate in a cool place for 2 hours.

Heat 2 tbsp oil in a heavy-based pan and sauté the whole dried red chillies for 1 minute. Add the lamb with its marinade and cook on a low heat for 45 minutes, or until the meat is cooked.

Meanwhile, heat the remaining 3 tbsp oil in another pan and sauté the whole spices and crushed peppercorns for a minute until they splutter. Add the rice and sauté for 2 minutes, then add 1.5 litres cold water. Bring to the boil and boil for 12–15 minutes until the rice is almost cooked.

Preheat the oven to 180°C (160°C fan oven) mark 4. Drain the rice and spread to a 2.5cm thickness on a tray. Allow to cool slightly, then pick out the cassia or cinnamon, cardamom pods and cloves.

In the meantime, deep-fry the thinly sliced onion until crisp and brown; drain on kitchen paper. Deep-fry the nuts, and raisins if using, until the nuts are light brown and the raisins are plump; drain.

Brush another heavy-based pan with a little melted butter and add half of the cooked lamb in a single layer. Cover with a layer of rice, 2.5cm thick, and sprinkle with garam masala and butter. Repeat these layers once more, then drizzle the saffron milk over the top layer of rice. Scatter the fried nuts and crisp-fried onion over the surface, cover tightly and place in the oven for 20 minutes. Uncover, fork through to mix, then sprinkle with the mint and coriander leaves. Serve at once, garnished with tomato strips and accompanied by the raita.

Cucumber and mint raita: Lightly whisk 200g Greek yogurt, then stir in ¼ tsp salt, ½ tsp toasted cumin seeds, 1 tbsp diced red onion, 1 tbsp chopped mint leaves and 1 tbsp grated, peeled cucumber.

500g lean boneless leg of lamb

MARINADE:
6 medium onions, finely sliced
oil, to deep-fry
200g natural set yogurt, whisked
1 tbsp ginger-garlic paste*
1 tsp ground turmeric
1 tsp salt

TO COOK:
5 tbsp vegetable oil
3 dried red chillies
5cm cassia bark or cinnamon stick
6 green cardamom pods
1 tsp cumin seeds
4 cloves
10 black peppercorns, crushed
500g basmati rice, washed and drained

TO ASSEMBLE:
1 small onion, thinly sliced
2 tbsp mixed almonds, cashew nuts and
    raisins (optional)
3 tbsp melted butter
2 tsp garam masala
pinch of saffron threads, infused in 100ml
    warm milk
1 tbsp finely chopped mint leaves
1 tbsp chopped coriander leaves

TO SERVE:
tomato strips, to garnish
cucumber and mint raita (see left)

BOLINAS DE CARNE EM CARIL VERDE

Goan lamb meat ball green curry GOA, WEST INDIA

The key to a good meat ball curry is a smooth mince with subtle spicing – the flavour of the meat should shine through the spices.

First soak the tamarind pulp for the coriander paste in 5 tbsp warm water for 20 minutes.

Meanwhile, mix together the ingredients for the meat balls in a bowl until evenly blended, then shape into small balls, the size of a walnut.

To make the coriander paste, strain the tamarind through a fine sieve and tip the liquid into a blender or mini-processor. Add the chopped coriander, salt, green chillies and ginger, and whiz to a paste; set aside.

For the sauce, heat the oil in a deep sauté pan. Add the garlic and sauté briefly, then add the onions and sauté until softened and light brown in colour. Add the ground coriander and cumin, and sauté for 30 seconds, then add the coconut milk and bring to a simmer.

Stir in the coriander paste and simmer gently for 3–5 minutes. Add the meat balls and simmer slowly for about 20 minutes until they are cooked.

In the meantime, toast the ingredients for the spice powder in a heavy-based frying pan over a medium heat for 2–3 minutes until they crackle, shaking the pan constantly. Cool slightly, then grind to a powder, using a spice grinder, mini-processor or pestle and mortar.

Sprinkle the toasted spice powder over the meat ball curry and simmer for 5 minutes. Serve with boiled rice.

MEAT BALLS:

500g lean boneless leg of lamb, finely minced

50g fresh breadcrumbs

1 tsp toasted cumin seeds, ground

pinch of mace powder

½ tsp salt

CORIANDER PASTE:

30g tamarind pulp*

6 tbsp chopped coriander leaves

1 tsp salt

3 green chillies

1 tbsp chopped root ginger

SAUCE:

1½ tbsp vegetable oil

1 tsp finely chopped garlic

150g onions, finely chopped

½ tsp ground coriander

½ tsp ground cumin

300ml coconut milk*

TOASTED SPICE POWDER:

6 peppercorns

2.5cm cinnamon stick

4 green cardamom pods

HIRAN TARIWALA

Venison with winter vegetables EAST INDIA

This warming dish is based on an old family recipe that my father used to cook lamb. I find it works well with venison and has been a favourite on my winter menus for several years.

Cut the venison into 2.5cm cubes. Pound the whole spices together using a pestle and mortar or spice grinder until coarsely ground.

Heat the oil in a deep heavy-based pan, add the pounded spices and stir until the mixture changes colour and crackles. Add the chopped onions and sauté until softened and golden brown.

Add the ginger-garlic paste and cook, stirring constantly, for 2–3 minutes – keep scraping the bottom of the pan to avoid burning.

Add the venison and sauté to seal on all sides, taking care not to burn the onions. Stir in the ground spices (except the garam masala). Cook over a low heat for about 30 minutes until the venison is three-quarters cooked.

In the meantime, whiz the tomatoes to a purée in a blender and sieve to remove seeds (if preferred); set aside. Blanch the vegetables separately in boiling salted water for 3–5 minutes until *al dente*; drain.

Add the puréed tomatoes to the venison, stir, then add the blanched vegetables. Cook gently for a further 15 minutes or until the venison is tender. Sprinkle with the garam masala and chopped coriander to serve.

600g boneless leg of venison, trimmed
1 cinnamon stick
4 cloves
6 green cardamom pods
1 tsp whole black peppercorns
1½ tsp cumin seeds
6 tbsp vegetable oil
3 medium onions, finely chopped
3 tsp ginger-garlic paste*
1 tbsp red chilli powder
1 tbsp ground coriander
1 tbsp ground turmeric
100g tomatoes
100g French beans, cut into 5cm lengths
12 baby turnips, scraped
12 baby carrots, scraped
20 button onions, peeled
salt
½ tsp garam masala
chopped coriander leaves, to garnish

PANDI KARI

Mangalorean pork curry SOUTH INDIA

This curry from Coorg also works well with lamb and venison.

Cut the pork into 2.5cm cubes and place in a shallow dish. Sprinkle with the salt, turmeric and vinegar and set aside to marinate for 30 minutes.

In the meantime, soak the tamarind in 150ml water warm water for 20 minutes, then strain through a fine sieve and set aside.

Transfer the pork and marinade to a heavy-based pan, add 200ml water and bring to a simmer. Cook gently for about 20 minutes.

Meanwhile, whiz the coriander, chillies, coconut, ginger, garlic, curry leaves and mango together in a blender or mini-processor to a fine paste.

Heat the oil in a deep sauté pan and sauté the mustard seeds until they crackle. Add the chopped onions and sauté until softened and light brown.

Add the pork, with its liquid, and cook for 15 minutes. Add the coriander and coconut paste and cook on a low heat for a further 5 minutes. Add the tamarind liquid and cook for another 5 minutes or until the pork is done. Adjust the seasoning. Scatter with the fried curry leaves and serve with rice.

500g lean boneless leg of pork
1 tsp salt
1 tsp ground turmeric
30ml vinegar
60g tamarind pulp*
30g coriander leaves, roughly chopped
2 green chillies
5 tbsp grated fresh coconut*
3 tbsp roughly chopped root ginger
8 garlic cloves, peeled
20 curry leaves, plus an extra 10 deep-fried leaves to garnish
30g mango flesh, or 2 tsp mango powder*
60ml vegetable oil
½ tsp black mustard seeds
150g onions, chopped

VEGETABLES AND PULSES

With a population that's over 80% vegetarian, a climate that promotes vegetables and pulses, and strong regional influences, it is not surprising that India's vegetarian cuisine is so rich and varied. Basic vegetables are cooked in hundreds of different ways across India, and in markets you find exotic varieties, such as drumsticks, gourds and unusual greens that are little known outside India. To me, vegetarian cooking is particularly challenging because the flavours are delicate, so the spicing must be very carefully balanced. Here is a spectrum of vegetable dishes from the different regions.

SING VATANA BATATA

Drumstick, pea and potato curry KHOJA, WEST INDIA

Drumsticks are a common vegetable in India. They look like long ridged beans (see photograph on page 104), but they are actually the unripe seed pods of a tree native to north-west India. Fortunately they are not hard to find in western markets. If you are unfamiliar with drumsticks, the way to savour them is to suck the pulp from the pods, then discard them – rather than eat them whole like beans. If you cannot find drumsticks, use French beans instead – I have found these work well with this recipe.

Cut the drumsticks into 2.5cm lengths. Blanch fresh peas in boiling salted water for 3–4 minutes, then drain. Cut the potatoes into wedges.

Put all the ingredients for the spice paste in a blender or mini-processor and whiz to a fine paste.

Heat the 2 tbsp oil in a wok or kadhai. Add the mustard seeds and curry leaves and sauté until they crackle, then add the spice paste and sauté for 3–4 minutes until the oil leaves the masala.

Add the drumsticks and potatoes, sauté for a few minutes, then add 100ml water and season with salt. Simmer for 20 minutes or until the drumsticks and potatoes are just cooked. Add the blanched (or frozen) peas and simmer for 2–3 minutes until tender. Serve hot.

200g drumsticks

100g shelled fresh or frozen peas

salt

180g Jersey Royal new potatoes, scrubbed

2 tbsp oil

1 tsp black mustard seeds

10 curry leaves

SPICE PASTE:

50g grated fresh coconut*

2 tbsp chopped coriander leaves

3 medium tomatoes

2 garlic cloves, peeled

2 tsp chopped root ginger

1 tbsp oil

1 tsp red chilli powder

½ tsp ground coriander

½ tsp ground cumin

½ tsp ground turmeric

BEGUN PORA

Roasted aubergine mash BENGAL, EAST INDIA

This flavoured aubergine mash makes a great accompaniment to any spicy curry; it can also be served chilled as a salad. At my restaurant, I serve it with my favourite lamb rack roast – it's a perfect match.

Preheat the oven to 200°C (180°C fan oven) mark 6. Brush the aubergine with a little of the oil and roast in the hot oven for about 15–20 minutes until the skin is charred and peels off easily. Leave until the aubergine is cool enough to handle, then peel away the skin, chop the pulp and tip into a bowl. Add the remaining oil and mash roughly, using a fork.

Add the onion, ginger, chilli, cumin and salt, and mix well. Finally add the lime juice and chopped coriander and toss to mix. Serve warm or chilled.

1 aubergine, about 400g

3 tbsp vegetable oil or olive oil

½ medium onion, finely chopped

1 tsp finely chopped root ginger

1 green chilli, finely chopped

½ tsp toasted cumin seeds, crushed

½ tsp salt, or to taste

1 tbsp lime juice

1 tbsp finely chopped coriander leaves

KALLA VEETU KATHRIKKAI

Chettiar aubergine curry TAMIL NADU, SOUTH INDIA

**As a child, I hated eating aubergine in curry form, then I was
introduced to this recipe in southern India at my hostel cafeteria –
and loved it. The amazing combination of flavours enhances mild
aubergine delightfully.**

Cut the baby aubergines in half lengthways. Cut the potatoes into wedges
and par-boil in salted water for 8–10 minutes, then drain.

Meanwhile, heat the oil in a wok or kadhai and sauté the cassia or
cinnamon, fennel seeds and curry leaves for a minute or two until they
crackle. Add the onions and garlic, and sauté until the onions are softened
and browned, then add the crushed chillies and coriander seeds and sauté
for 1–2 minutes.

Add the aubergines and potatoes, and cook for few minutes until the
aubergines soften. Add the tomato, coconut milk, 100ml water and salt to
taste. Bring to a simmer and cook gently for about 10 minutes until the
vegetables are cooked and the sauce has thickened.

Scatter with chopped coriander leaves to serve.

8–10 baby aubergines

3 medium potatoes

salt

4 tbsp vegetable oil

5cm cassia bark or cinnamon stick

1 tsp fennel seeds

8 curry leaves

2 large onions, finely chopped

1½ tsp finely chopped garlic

10 dried red chillies, crushed

3 tbsp toasted coriander seeds, crushed

1 large tomato, cut into wedges

400ml coconut milk*

2 tbsp chopped coriander leaves

DAHAIWALE ALOO GOBI

Cauliflower and potato curry BIHAR, EAST INDIA

Cooking with yogurt is an ancient technique in India. I have fond memories of this recipe – the *littee* vendor in my home town sold an exceptionally good version. Indeed *littee* (page 16) are an excellent accompaniment, perfect for mopping up the delicious cooking liquor.

Cut the potatoes into wedges. Cut the cauliflower into small florets. Heat the oil in a sauté pan and lightly fry the potato wedges and cauliflower, turning, for 3–5 minutes. Remove and set aside.

Add the nigella or onion seeds, cloves, cardamom pods, cassia or cinnamon and bay leaf to the oil remaining in the pan, and sauté for a minute or two until the spices crackle.

Return the potatoes and cauliflower to the pan and add the turmeric, chilli powder, salt and sugar. Mix well and add 300ml water. Bring to the boil, lower the heat and simmer for about 20 minutes until the potatoes are just cooked.

Add the tomatoes and yogurt, bring to a simmer and cook for 5 minutes. Add the chopped coriander and sprinkle with garam masala to serve.

2 medium potatoes, peeled

1 medium cauliflower, trimmed

3 tbsp vegetable oil or mustard oil

1 tsp nigella or onion seeds

2 cloves

2 cardamom pods

2.5cm cassia bark or cinnamon stick

1 bay leaf

1 tsp ground turmeric

½ tsp red chilli powder

1 tsp salt

1 tsp sugar

2 medium tomatoes, cut into wedges

200g yogurt, lightly whisked

1 tbsp coriander leaves, finely chopped

½ tsp garam masala

KEERAI PORIYAL

Stir-fried spinach SOUTH INDIA

In Tamil Nadu, *arrakeerai* and *sirukeerai* are the two greens stir-fried in this way, but the result is equally good with plain spinach. The equivalent dishes in Kerala are called *thoran*. The principle is the same, though the *thoran* seasoning technique is a little different.

Wash the spinach, drain well and shred the leaves; set aside.

Heat the oil in a wok or kadhai and sauté the mustard seeds and black gram with the garlic and whole red chillies until they crackle. Add the chopped onion and sauté until translucent and softened.

Add the shredded spinach and season with salt. Cook on a low heat for a few minutes until the spinach is just wilted and any liquid has evaporated. Sprinkle with the grated coconut to serve.

500g spinach leaves
1 tbsp vegetable oil
½ tsp black mustard seeds
½ tsp split black gram*
6 garlic cloves, finely chopped
2 dried red chillies
1 small onion, finely chopped
½ tsp salt, or to taste
3 tbsp grated fresh coconut*

SAAG PANEER

Spinach with fried paneer NORTH INDIA

Saag paneer is a special winter preparation in north Indian homes, reserved for visiting guests. This recipe is a source of pride for Indian housewives, so if you happen to be that lucky guest, don't compare it to other *saag paneers* you have tasted – you would be asking for trouble. Cooking is a serious matter of unpredictable jealousy among Indian housewives.

Wash the spinach, drain well and roughly chop the leaves; set aside. Cut the paneer into 2cm cubes. Heat the oil for deep-frying in a large, deep pan to 180°C and deep-fry the paneer cubes in batches for about 1 minute to seal and lightly colour the surface. Drain on kitchen paper.

Heat the butter and 2 tbsp oil in a sauté pan, add the garlic and sauté for 1–2 minutes until golden brown. Add the cumin seeds and sauté for a minute until they start crackling. Add the red chilli powder and ground coriander and stir for a further 1 minute.

Add the spinach and cook over a low heat for 10 minutes, stirring constantly until the leaves wilt.

Add the paneer cubes, ginger and salt, and cook slowly for 5–7 minutes. As the oil starts to shine on the surface of the spinach, stir in the cream.

Sprinkle with garam masala and serve garnished with tomato strips.

1kg spinach leaves
300g paneer cheese
vegetable oil, to deep-fry, plus 2 tbsp
2 tbsp butter
2 tsp finely chopped garlic
1 tsp cumin seeds
1 tsp red chilli powder
1 tsp ground coriander
2 tsp finely chopped ginger
1 tsp salt
2 tbsp single cream
1 tsp garam masala
1 medium tomato, cut into thin strips, to garnish

SINGHORA DIYE KOLMI SAAG BHAJI

Sautéed watercress with water chestnuts EAST INDIA

Watercress and water chestnuts are both abundant in the markets of Calcutta. Their flavours and textures marry perfectly, giving a natural spicy edge. This recipe is probably the result of neighbouring influences on Bengali cuisine from countries like Mynamar, and the Chinese community of Calcutta.

Rinse the watercress, pat dry and set aside. Heat the mustard oil in a wok or kadhai. Add the nigella and fennel seeds and sauté until they crackle, then add the garlic and sauté briefly until light brown in colour.

Add the water chestnuts and sauté for 1 minute, then stir in the turmeric and chilli powder. Add the watercress to the pan with the salt. Cook on a low heat for a minute, until the leaves just wilt. Serve immediately.

500g watercress, tough stalks removed
1 tbsp mustard oil
1/2 tsp nigella seeds
1/4 tsp fennel seeds
2 garlic cloves, crushed
250g canned water chestnuts, drained
and sliced
1/4 tsp ground turmeric
1/4 tsp red chilli powder
1/2 tsp salt, or to taste

DHAROSH CHACHHARI

Spicy dry okra EAST INDIA

Cooking with mustard paste and mustard oil is an acquired taste, but one you can easily take on. Either use an authentic Indian mustard paste or buy one of the mild mustard pastes available – for a similar flavour with less pungency. This dish can be garnished with crisp-fried okra if you like.

Slit the okra from tip to tail and set aside. Soak the tamarind pulp in 3 tbsp warm water for 20 minutes, then strain through a fine sieve.

Heat the oil in a wok or kadhai, add the onion seeds and sauté until they crackle. Add the okra and sauté for a minute.

Add the chilli powder, turmeric, salt and sugar. Cook over a low heat for 12–15 minutes until the okra is tender. Mix the mustard paste with the tamarind liquid and add to the pan. Cook, stirring gently, for 2–3 minutes, then check the seasoning and serve.

500g okra, washed
10g tamarind pulp*
2 tsp vegetable or mustard oil
1/4 tsp onion seeds
1 tsp chilli powder
1 tsp ground turmeric
1/2 tsp salt, or to taste
1/4 tsp sugar
2 tsp mustard seed paste*,
or Dijon mustard

CHINA BODAM DIYE LAL SAAG

Red chard with coriander and peanuts CALCUTTA, EAST INDIA

A variety of red spinach is sold in Calcutta's vegetable markets. Red chard is a good alternative and works very well in this recipe.

Remove the stems from the chard or spinach and wash the leaves; drain well. Lightly toast the coriander seeds and dried red chilli together in a small heavy-based frying pan over a medium heat for a minute or two until they begin to crackle, shaking the pan constantly. Crush finely, using a mini-processor or pestle and mortar.

Heat the mustard oil in a wok or deep sauté pan, add the crushed coriander and chilli mixture and sauté for 1 minute. Add the chopped garlic and sauté until golden brown in colour.

Add the sliced onion and sauté until softened, then add the tomatoes, stir and add the turmeric. Cook on a low heat for a couple of minutes.

Add the chard or spinach leaves to the pan with the salt and cook on a low heat for a few minutes until all the moisture has evaporated and the chard leaves start to wilt. Add the crushed peanuts, toss to mix and remove from the heat. Serve at once.

800g young red chard or spinach leaves
1½ tsp coriander seeds
1 dried red chilli
2 tbsp mustard oil or vegetable oil
1 garlic clove, chopped
1 medium onion, finely sliced
3 medium tomatoes, chopped
1 tsp ground turmeric
½ tsp salt, or to taste
2 tbsp unsalted peanuts, toasted
   and crushed

MUTTAKOS KARAT THOREN

Stir-fried cabbage and carrot with coconut SOUTH INDIA

Thoran, poriyal, kaalan, palya and *foogath* **are simply different names used to describe this kind of dish in different parts of India. The principles of cooking and spicing are similar. All are vegetable-based and feature coconut, curry leaves and mustard seeds. Perhaps they are best described as warm salads. Fresh coconut is essential here.**

Shred the cabbage and grate the carrots or cut into julienne; set aside.

Heat the oil in a wok or kadhai. Add the mustard seeds and, as they splutter, add the black gram and fry until golden brown in colour. Add the sliced onion, green chillies and curry leaves, and sauté until the onion is softened and translucent.

Add the grated coconut and sauté lightly, without colouring, to extract the flavour. Add the shredded cabbage, carrot, sprouted beans if using, and salt. Cook gently for 10–15 minutes until the vegetables are just cooked. Serve immediately.

400g white cabbage, cored
70g carrots
2 tbsp vegetable oil
1 tsp black mustard seeds
2 tsp black gram*
1 medium onion, thinly sliced
2 green chillies, slit lengthways
10 curry leaves
150g grated fresh coconut*
50g green mung beans, sprouted
   (optional)
½ tsp salt, or to taste

FULAVER GAJJAR VATANA NU SHAK

Spiced cauliflower, carrots and peas GUJARAT, WEST INDIA

Among Indian regional cuisine, I believe Gujarati food stands out for its ingenious spicing techniques and the melange of colours and textures. This recipe is a regular feature in Gujarati homes – its simple, bold flavours shine through perfectly.

Cut the cauliflower into small florets. If using fresh peas, blanch in boiling salted water for 3–4 minutes, then drain. Blanch the diced carrots in boiling water for 3 minutes; drain.

Meanwhile, heat the oil in a wok or kadhai. Add the asafoetida and mustard seeds, and sauté for a minute or two until the seeds splutter. Add the green chillies, cauliflower florets and ½ tsp salt. Cook over a low heat for about 10 minutes until the cauliflower stems soften. Add the blanched (or frozen) peas, carrots and powdered spices. Cook for a few minutes until the vegetables are tender.

Serve in warmed bowls, scattered with shredded coriander leaves and accompanied by Indian breads.

300g cauliflower, trimmed
100g shelled fresh or frozen peas
salt
100g carrots, diced
2 tbsp vegetable oil
pinch of asafoetida*
½ tsp black mustard seeds
2 green chillies, slit lengthways
¼ tsp ground cumin
¼ tsp ground coriander
½ tsp red chilli powder
½ tsp ground turmeric
2 tbsp shredded coriander leaves

PATTAR KOLU ANE GUVAR FALI NU SHAK

Pumpkin and cluster bean curry GUJARAT, WEST INDIA

The sweet flavours of the vegetables are perfectly balanced by the spices in this recipe. If you are not keen on cluster beans, you could use French beans instead.

Cut the pumpkin into 2.5cm long batons. Cut the cluster or French beans into 2.5cm lengths.

Bring 200ml water to the boil in a pan. Add the pumpkin, beans, oil and salt. Bring to the boil, lower the heat and simmer for about 3–5 minutes until the beans are just softened.

Add the powdered spices and sugar, and continue to cook on a low heat for 2–3 minutes until the vegetables are tender. Serve sprinkled with chopped coriander leaves.

200g yellow pumpkin, skin removed
    and deseeded
100g cluster beans or French beans
2 tbsp vegetable oil
½ tsp salt, or to taste
½ tsp ground turmeric
½ tsp red chilli powder
½ tsp ground cumin
½ tsp ground coriander
20g palm sugar or jaggery*
2 tsp chopped coriander leaves

ALOO PIAJ KOLI O TOMATOR TORKARI

Spring onions with potatoes and tomatoes EAST INDIA

This recipe is a prime example of minimalist Bengali cooking. Small amounts of spices are used, so the fresh flavours of the vegetables and coriander shine through. No water is added to this dish.

Cut the spring onions into 5cm lengths and set aside.

Heat the oil in a wok or deep frying pan to smoking point, then reduce the heat to medium and add the panch phoran. Stir for 1 minute or until the spices change colour, then add the potatoes and sliced onions. Cook, stirring, for 2–3 minutes, then add the tomatoes.

Sprinkle in the turmeric, salt and sugar, stir well and reduce the heat to low. Cover the pan and cook for 8–10 minutes, until the potatoes are almost cooked.

Add the spring onions and cook for a further 3–5 minutes until the spring onions and potatoes are tender and the oil starts to separate. Serve garnished with coriander sprigs.

1 bunch of spring onions, trimmed

2 tbsp mustard oil or vegetable oil

1 tsp panch phoran*

20 new potatoes, quartered

2 medium onions, thinly sliced

2 medium tomatoes, thinly sliced

1 tsp ground turmeric

1 tsp salt, or to taste

1/2 tsp sugar

coriander sprigs, to garnish

TETUL DIYE SHEEMER TORKARI

Broad beans with tamarind   BENGAL, EAST INDIA

Broad beans are an everyday vegetable in west Bengal. This is a recipe with minimal cooking and spicing, and it's therefore fast to prepare. Indian broad beans have softer pods than those generally available in this country and they can be cooked whole. You may be lucky enough to find tender broad beans in pods early in the season, otherwise substitute French beans for this recipe.

Blanch the broad beans in boiling salted water for about 3–4 minutes until *al dente*. Drain and immerse the beans in a bowl of ice-cold water to refresh. When cold, remove and set aside. Soak the tamarind pulp in 6 tbsp warm water for 20 minutes, then strain through a fine sieve.

Heat the oil in a wok or deep frying pan. Add the nigella and cumin seeds, and sauté until they crackle. Add the sliced chillies and ginger strips, and sauté until the chillies have softened.

Add the sliced broad beans and sauté for 1 minute, then sprinkle in the turmeric, sugar and salt to taste, and cook for another minute. Add the tamarind liquid and stir well. Serve garnished with ginger julienne.

400g young broad beans in the pod, or
　French beans, sliced diagonally
salt
30g tamarind pulp*
2 tbsp mustard oil or vegetable oil
½ tsp nigella seeds
½ tsp cumin seeds
2 green chillies, sliced diagonally
1 knob of root ginger, cut into thin strips
½ tsp ground turmeric
2 tsp sugar
ginger julienne, to garnish

KANDE KI SUBJI

Spicy onions RAJASTHAN, NORTH INDIA

In Rajasthan, onion is an essential food and it is cooked in various ways. This simple recipe makes a great accompaniment to almost any meal. Serve an Indian bread alongside.

Cut the red and white onions into thick slices. Cut the white part of the spring onions into thick strips. Cut the green part into julienne and set aside for the garnish.

Heat the 3 tbsp oil in a wok or kadhai and sauté the cumin seeds until they splutter. Add the ginger-garlic paste and sauté for 2–3 minutes until well cooked.

Add the powdered spices, salt, 3 tbsp water and the yogurt. Cook this mixture well, stirring, for 3–4 minutes, then add the onions, including the white spring onion and stir-fry for about 5–7 minutes until they are just cooked, but retaining a bite.

In the meantime, heat the oil for deep-frying in a deep-fryer or other suitable pan to 180°C and deep-fry the shredded green spring onion for about 20–30 seconds until crisp. Drain on kitchen paper.

Serve the onions in bowls, topped with the fried spring onion greens.

150g red onions

150g white onions

100g spring onions, trimmed

3 tbsp vegetable oil, plus oil to deep-fry

½ tsp cumin seeds

2 tsp ginger-garlic paste*

1 tsp red chilli powder

1 tsp ground coriander

½ tsp ground turmeric

½ tsp salt, or to taste

2 tbsp yogurt

DHANIYAE AUR PYAZ KI KHUMBI

Mushrooms with coriander leaves NORTH INDIA

I must have inherited my love of mushrooms from my mother; this is her recipe and I have eaten it zillions of times. She makes it with button mushrooms and *dhingri* (Indian shiitake), but I use a mixture of varieties. It is an ideal accompaniment to many chicken dishes.

Slice the mushrooms and cut the spring onions into julienne strips.

Heat 2 tbsp oil in a sauté pan, add half of the chopped garlic and sauté for 2 minutes until light brown in colour. Add the coriander seeds and red chilli, and sauté for a minute, then add the tomatoes and salt. Cook for about 10 minutes until the tomatoes are just softened.

Heat the remaining 1 tbsp oil in a wok and sauté the rest of the garlic for 1–2 minutes. Add the mushrooms and spring onions, and sprinkle with the turmeric and black pepper. Sauté for 3–4 minutes until the mushrooms just soften. Add the tomato mixture and sauté for a further 3–4 minutes. Serve at once, sprinkled with coriander leaves.

400g mixed mushrooms (shiitake, oyster, chestnut etc)

4 spring onions, white part only

3 tbsp vegetable oil

2 tsp finely chopped garlic

1 tsp coriander seeds, crushed

1 small dried red chilli, crushed

2 medium tomatoes, finely chopped

½ tsp salt, or to taste

½ tsp ground turmeric

¼ tsp black peppercorns, crushed

3 tbsp coriander leaves

SHALGAM MASALA

Turnips with ginger and nigella seeds PUNJAB, NORTH INDIA

Baby turnips are used as a salad ingredient in Punjabi villages, along with mooli and carrots. These root vegetables are used in various forms in India; they are even sun-dried to ensure a year-round supply. I came across a recipe like this made with large turnips and promptly turned it into a baby turnip recipe; it works well and doesn't require lengthy cooking.

Cut the baby turnips into quarters. Heat the oil in a sauté pan, add the nigella seeds, green chilli and ginger, and sauté for 1–2 minutes until the seeds crackle.

Add the turnips and powdered spices, and sauté over a low heat for 3 minutes. Add the chopped tomato and salt. Cover and cook until the turnips are soft.

Sprinkle the garam masala, chopped coriander and ginger julienne over the turnips and serve.

300g baby turnips, cleaned
2 tbsp vegetable oil
1 tsp nigella seeds
1 green chilli, chopped
1/2 tsp chopped root ginger
1 tsp ground turmeric
1/4 tsp red chilli powder
1 tsp ground coriander
1 medium tomato, chopped
1/2 tsp salt, or to taste
1/4 tsp garam masala
1 tbsp chopped coriander leaves
5g root ginger julienne

GANTH GOBI

Kashmiri kohlrabi NORTH INDIA

Kohlrabi is a common vegetable in Kashmir, but not in other parts of India. I have often seen *khol–khol*, as Kashmiri call it, in New Delhi and Jaipur vegetable markets; I presume locals buy it mainly to prepare salads or pickles.

Peel the kohlrabi and cut into wedges. Heat the oil in a sauté pan. Add the asafoetida and sauté until it sizzles, then add the cumin, fenugreek seeds and cloves. Sauté for 1–2 minutes until the spices crackle.

Add the kohlrabi and sauté for 2–3 minutes, then lower the heat and add 2–3 tbsp water. Cover and cook for a few minutes.

Add the chilli, ginger, powdered spices and salt. Sauté for 30 seconds or so to cook the spices and then add 100ml water. Cook over a low heat for 10–15 minutes until the kohlrabi is soft. Add the sugar and chopped coriander leaves and cook until the water evaporates. Serve hot.

500g kohlrabi
5 tbsp vegetable oil or ghee*
pinch of asafoetida*
1/2 tsp cumin seeds
1/4 tsp fenugreek seeds
2 cloves
1 green chilli, chopped
1 tsp chopped root ginger
1/4 tsp red chilli powder
1 tsp ground coriander
1/2 tsp garam masala
1/4 tsp ground ginger
1 tsp ground turmeric
1/2 tsp salt, or to taste
1/2 tsp sugar
1 tbsp chopped coriander leaves

ALOO DUM

Potatoes cooked with melon seeds NORTH INDIA

There are numerous different recipes for this dish – this simple north Indian preparation, enriched with yogurt, is from the Mogulai cuisine.

Put the melon seeds or cashew nuts in a bowl, add warm water to cover and soak for 10 minutes, then drain and grind to a fine paste, using a blender or mini-processor; remove and set aside.

Heat a 2cm depth of oil in a pan and fry the onions until softened and light brown in colour. Remove with a slotted spoon and drain on kitchen paper; leave to cool. Add the potatoes to the hot oil and fry for 3–4 minutes until golden brown; remove and drain on kitchen paper.

Whiz the fried onions in a blender or mini-processor to a paste, add the yogurt and process until smooth; remove and set aside.

Heat the 3 tbsp oil in a sauté pan and sauté the ginger and garlic until golden brown. Add the ground spices and sauté for a few seconds, then stir in the yogurt and onion paste. Whisk in the seed or nut paste and bring the sauce to a simmer, stirring. Add the potatoes, 150ml water and the salt. Bring to a simmer and cook for 15 minutes or until the potatoes are tender.

In the meantime, toast the ingredients for the spice powder in a heavy-based frying pan over a medium heat for 2–3 minutes until they crackle, shaking the pan constantly. Cool slightly, then grind to a powder, using a spice grinder, mini-processor or pestle and mortar.

Add the toasted spice blend and chopped coriander to the potatoes, stir and take off the heat. Serve in bowls, garnished with coriander sprigs.

2 tbsp melon seeds or cashew nuts

3 tbsp vegetable oil, plus extra to shallow-fry

2 medium onions, thinly sliced

500g baby new potatoes, peeled

200g yogurt

1½ tsp chopped root ginger

1 tsp chopped garlic

½ tsp ground coriander

½ tsp chilli powder

½ tsp ground cumin

1 tsp salt

1 tbsp chopped coriander leaves, plus extra sprigs to garnish

TOASTED SPICE POWDER:

3 black cardamom pods

½ tsp fennel seeds

5cm cassia bark or cinnamon stick

URULAI SOYIKEERAI VARIYAL

Sautéed potatoes with dill leaves SOUTH INDIA

Dill leaves marry with the spices in this recipe to enhance the flavour of new potatoes. It's a simple, quick dish – perfect instant food.

Par-boil the potatoes in salted water for 5 minutes, then drain. When cool enough to handle, peel and cut into quarters.

Heat the oil in a sauté pan, add the mustard and sesame seeds, and sauté until they splutter. Add the peanuts and sauté until golden brown. Add the onion and sauté until softened and light brown in colour. Add the powdered spices, ½ tsp salt and the chopped ginger and cook for a few minutes, stirring and taking care to avoid burning.

Add the chopped tomato and dill, and sauté to allow the dill leaves to blend well with the spices. Add the potatoes and cook for 10 minutes or until they are tender and coated with the spice mixture and dill leaves.

400g Jersey Royal new potatoes, scrubbed

salt

2 tbsp vegetable oil

½ tsp black mustard seeds

½ tsp sesame seeds

1 tbsp peanuts

1 small onion, chopped

½ tsp ground turmeric

1½ tsp ground coriander

1 tsp red chilli powder

1 tsp chopped root ginger

1 tomato, chopped

3 tbsp chopped dill leaves

MULANGI KADALAI KOZHAMBU

Radish and chickpea curry TAMIL NADU, SOUTH INDIA

Mooli or daikon with its fresh peppery taste is a favoured vegetable in India. I find it works well with this combination of flavourings.

Drain the chickpeas and cook in fresh water with the bay leaf for about 2 hours until tender, adding salt towards the end; drain. Soak the tamarind pulp in 6 tbsp warm water for 20 minutes, then strain through a fine sieve.

Halve the mooli lengthways, then cut across into 5mm thick slices. Heat the oil in a sauté pan and fry the mooli slices until lightly browned at the edges; remove and drain on kitchen paper.

Add the whole spices to the pan and sauté for 1–2 minutes until they crackle. Add the onion and sauté until softened and golden brown.

Add the powdered spices, stir for 30 seconds, then add the ginger-garlic paste and sauté well for 2–3 minutes.

Add the tomato and cook for about 10 minutes. Stir in the tamarind liquid, simmer briefly, then add the coconut milk, chickpeas and mooli. Bring to a simmer and cook for 3–5 minutes until the mooli is tender. Sprinkle with the chopped coriander and serve garnished with extra sprigs.

200g chickpeas, soaked in cold water overnight
1 bay leaf
1 tsp salt, or to taste
30g tamarind pulp*
200g mooli or daikon (white radish)
2 tbsp oil
2 cloves
2.5cm cassia bark or cinnamon stick
2 green cardamom pods
1 large onion, chopped
½ tsp ground turmeric
1 tsp red chilli powder
¾ tsp ground coriander
2 tsp ginger-garlic paste*
1 tomato, finely chopped
300ml coconut milk*
1 tbsp chopped coriander leaves, plus extra sprigs

PAPPU DOSAKAI

Pumpkin with lentils ANDHRA PRADESH, SOUTH INDIA

Cooking lentils with different varieties of squash is common in all four corners of India. Bottle gourd is typically used here, but butternut squash or yellow pumpkin would also hold good. This recipe is from a family in Guntur – home to some of India's finest chillies.

Peel and deseed the pumpkin or gourd and cut into 2.5cm dice. Cook the lentils in boiling salted water for about 20 minutes, until just turning soft but not completely cooked. Drain off all but a cupful of water.

Add the green chillies, pumpkin or gourd, onions and tomatoes. Simmer over a low heat for about 10 minutes until the pumpkin turns soft.

Add the chilli powder, toasted coriander, turmeric, chopped garlic and ½ tsp salt, and cook, stirring, for a few minutes. Stir in the coconut and simmer for 5 minutes, adding a little more water if necessary. Add the chopped coriander and remove from the heat.

Serve in bowls, garnished with fresh coconut slices if you like, and accompanied by Indian breads.

500g pumpkin or bottle gourd (dudi)

150g Bengal gram*

salt

2 green chillies, slit lengthways

2 onions, finely sliced

2 tomatoes, cut into wedges

1 tsp red chilli powder

½ tsp ground coriander, toasted

¼ tsp ground turmeric

½ tsp finely chopped garlic

4 tbsp grated fresh coconut*

4 tbsp chopped coriander leaves

thin slices of fresh coconut*, to garnish
  (optional)

TADKA DAL

Home-style lentils NORTH INDIA

**This lentil preparation is famous for it spicing, but it is the chilli and
garlic in the seasoning that provide the real kick. An effortless
recipe, this requires no forward planning.**

Put the split peas or dal into a saucepan with the salt, turmeric and 1 litre
water. Bring to the boil, lower the heat and simmer for 15–20 minutes until
the lentils are soft.

For the seasoning, heat the oil in a sauté pan and fry the garlic until light
brown in colour. Add the chilli powder and sauté for a minute. Add the
tomatoes and cook for 3–4 minutes, then add the cooked lentils. Simmer
for 10–15 minutes.

Serve the dal hot, sprinkled with shredded coriander leaves and crisp
deep-fried onions if you like.

300g yellow split peas or channa dal

1 tsp salt

1 tsp ground turmeric

SEASONING:

1 tbsp vegetable oil

1 tsp finely chopped garlic

1 tsp red chilli powder

2 medium tomatoes, chopped

GARNISH:

1 tsp shredded coriander leaves

deep-fried onions (optional)

CHANNA MASALA

Chickpeas from Punjab PUNJAB, NORTH INDIA

Pre-soaking pulses overnight – especially chickpeas, red kidney beans and lentils – is a common practice in India, to shorten cooking times the following day. This recipe is an all-time favourite in north India. It is usually paired with _bhatura_ – a bread similar to naan but deep-fried. I recommend serving sliced red onion, green chilli and mango pickle with this dish, too.

Drain the chickpeas, put into a saucepan and cover with 1 litre fresh water. Add the tea bag and bring to the boil. Lower the heat and simmer until the chickpeas are cooked, about 2 hours. Season with ½ tsp salt towards the end of cooking. Drain the chickpeas, reserving the liquid.

Heat the oil in a wok or kadhai and sauté the onions until softened and golden brown in colour. Add the garlic, ginger and chillies, and sauté for a minute or two until the garlic is golden.

Stir in the chopped tomatoes and cook for 10 minutes to soften a little. Stir in the coriander, cumin, turmeric and chilli powder, lower the heat and cook for 2 minutes or until the fat separates out from the onion mixture.

Add the chickpeas, a little more salt if required and 1 cup of the reserved liquid. Simmer for about 20 minutes or until the liquid is absorbed. Stir in 1 tbsp chopped coriander leaves.

Add the garam masala, crushed toasted cumin and coriander seeds. Sprinkle with the lemon juice, ginger julienne and remaining chopped coriander leaves to serve. Accompany with bhatura (page 136).

250g chickpeas, soaked in cold water
  overnight
1 tea bag
½ tsp salt, or to taste
3 tbsp vegetable oil
4 medium onions, chopped
2 tsp chopped garlic
1 tbsp chopped root ginger
3 green chillies, sliced
5 tomatoes, chopped
2 tsp ground coriander
1 tsp ground cumin
½ tsp ground turmeric
1 tsp red chilli powder
2 tbsp chopped coriander leaves
¼ tsp garam masala
1 tsp toasted cumin seeds, crushed
1 tsp toasted coriander seeds, crushed
1 tbsp lemon juice
1 tbsp root ginger julienne

[handwritten note: ? reduce qty of liquid quantities by ½ since chickpeas are already rehydrated (250g once drained)?]

AAMER DIYE TAWKER DAL

Spicy lentils with mango BENGAL, EAST INDIA

Lentil preparations are so versatile and so varied within India that there must be millions of recipes based on lentils alone. This recipe is a local favourite in west Bengal's villages. The natural flavour of ingredients is the main play in Bengali cuisine, and that's evident in this simple combination of mango and lentil.

Put the lentils in a saucepan with 800ml water, the turmeric, mango powder or sliced raw mango and salt. Bring to the boil and simmer for about 15–20 minutes until the lentils and raw mango if using, are cooked.

Heat the oil in a large sauté pan, add the mustard seeds and, as they begin to crackle, add the chillies, followed by the lentil and mango mixture. Cook for about 5 minutes until the liquid has reduced slightly.

Serve garnished with chopped coriander leaves.

250g split red lentils, washed
½ tsp ground turmeric
1 tbsp dried mango powder*, or 2 small
  green mangoes, peeled and sliced
1 tsp salt
1 tbsp mustard oil or vegetable oil
½ tsp black mustard seeds
3 green chillies
1 tbsp coriander leaves, chopped,
  to garnish

ACCOMPANIMENTS

Bread or rice is always at the heart of an Indian meal. In general, bread is the staple food in the north of India, while rice is more common in coastal India and particularly in the south. India produces various cereals, including corn, millet and barley, but the most popular north Indian breads – including chapattis and naan – are made from wheat flour. Of course, no Indian meal is complete without a chutney. Indians eat tangy, sweet or sour relishes with almost every meal and snack. Here you will find a good selection to accompany the appetisers and kebabs in the book.

NIRAMISH PULAO

Vegetarian rice BENARES, NORTH INDIA

I have always liked the food in the city of Benares. It is predominantly a Hindu city steeped in ancient traditions and the food is similarly well established. This interesting rice dish couldn't be easier to make.

Wash the basmati rice in several changes of cold water, then leave to soak in cold water to cover for 15–20 minutes. Drain the rice and set aside.

Whiz together the ingredients for the spice paste in a blender or mini-processor to make a fine paste; set aside.

Heat the butter and oil in a heavy-based pan and add the onions, cassia or cinnamon, cardamom pods and mace. Fry, stirring, until the onions are softened and golden brown in colour.

Add the peas and beans to the pan and sauté for 3–5 minutes, then add the chopped tomatoes. Add the spice paste and cook, stirring, for 2–3 minutes. Add the rice, 1 litre water and the salt. Bring to the boil, lower the heat and simmer for about 20 minutes until the rice is cooked and the water is absorbed. Serve hot.

500g basmati rice
1 tbsp butter
2 tsp vegetable oil
100g sliced onions
2.5cm cassia bark or cinnamon stick
2 black cardamom pods
1 mace blade
200g shelled peas
200g French beans, cut into 3cm batons
100g tomatoes, chopped
1 tsp salt, or to taste

SPICE PASTE:
½ tsp ground turmeric
10g root ginger, roughly chopped
50g coriander leaves

BANGALI PULAO

East Indian pulao EAST INDIA

This spicy rice preparation is especially popular during the festival of 'Durga Puja'. It is flavoured with an unusual blend of aromatics and spices. I like to serve it with a potato curry flavoured with bay leaves.

Wash the basmati rice in several changes of cold water, then leave to soak in cold water to cover for 1 hour. Drain the rice and set aside.

Heat the butter in a heavy-based pan or flameproof casserole and sauté the whole spices, nuts and raisins for a minute until the spices crackle. Add the rice and sauté for a minute.

Add 800ml water and stir in the garam masala, saffron threads, grated nutmeg, salt and sugar. Bring to the boil and boil for about 8–10 minutes until the rice on the surface is no longer wet, indicating that most of the water has been absorbed.

Lower the heat and cover the pan or casserole tightly. Simmer on the hob, or in the oven at 180°C (160°C fan oven) mark 4 for 10–12 minutes until the rice is cooked.

Uncover, sprinkle with the rose water and kewra if using, and fork through. Serve, garnished with rose petals and jasmine flowers if you like.

400g basmati rice
50g butter
5cm cassia bark or cinnamon stick
2 cloves
3 green cardamom pods
50g cashew nuts
25g raisins
1 tsp Bengali garam masala*
pinch of saffron threads
freshly grated nutmeg, to taste
1 tsp salt, or to taste
1 tsp sugar
1 tsp rose water
1 tsp kewra water or screwpine flower essence*
   (optional)
rose petals and jasmine flowers, to garnish (optional)

ARROZ COM COCO

Coconut rice   GOA, WEST INDIA

This is the universal rice for Goans and complements most curries of west Indian origin. In Goa, the local red rice would be used, but I find basmati rice works just as well.

Wash the basmati rice in several changes of cold water, then leave to soak in cold water to cover for 15–20 minutes. Drain and set aside.

Heat the oil in a large heavy-based pan and sauté the whole spices for a minute or two. Stir in the ginger-garlic paste and sauté for 2–3 minutes, then add the onions and cook until softened and golden brown. Add the turmeric and rice, and sauté for 2 minutes.

Stir in the coconut milk, salt and 100ml water. Bring to a simmer and cook for about 20 minutes until the rice is tender and the liquid is absorbed.

250g basmati rice

2 tbsp coconut oil or vegetable oil

2.5cm cassia bark or cinnamon stick

2 cloves

6–8 black peppercorns

3 green cardamom pods

½ tsp ginger-garlic paste*

100g onions, sliced

½ tsp ground turmeric

300ml coconut milk*

1 tsp salt

ELUMICHAMPAZHA SADAM

Lemon rice   SOUTH INDIA

Rice is the staple food in the south of India, and there are many interesting rice preparations from the region. With so many tasty ingredients, this recipe is stunning and it goes well with most of the south Indian main dishes in the preceding chapters.

Cook the rice in plenty of boiling salted water for about 20 minutes until just cooked. In the meantime, lightly toast the ingredients for the spice powder in a heavy-based frying pan over a medium heat for 1–2 minutes until they begin to crackle, shaking the pan constantly. Cool slightly, then grind to a powder, using a spice grinder, mini-processor or pestle and mortar; set aside. When cooked, drain the rice and set aside.

Heat the oil in a heavy-based pan and add the mustard and cumin seeds, black and Bengal gram, dried red chilli, asafoetida and curry leaves. As the mustard seeds pop, add the green chillies, ginger and peanuts. Sauté for 2–3 minutes.

Add the turmeric, rice and salt to taste. Stir over a low heat until heated through, then add the toasted spice powder and mix well. Remove from the heat and add the lemon juice. Scatter with chopped coriander to serve.

300g basmati rice

salt

2 tbsp vegetable oil

TOASTED SPICE POWDER:

½ tsp aniseed

2 green cardamom pods

1 clove

1cm cassia bark or cinnamon stick

½ tsp poppy seeds

SEASONING (TEMPERING):

1 tsp black mustard seeds

1 tsp cumin seeds

1 tsp each black gram* and Bengal gram*

1 dried red chilli

½ tsp asafoetida*

10 curry leaves

2 green chillies, chopped

1 tbsp finely chopped root ginger

3 tbsp peanuts

¼ tsp ground turmeric

juice of 2 lemons

2 tbsp chopped coriander leaves

MEETHE CHAWAL

Sweet rice   CENTRAL INDIA

Sweet rice is a Muslim tradition in India. Muslim communities in different parts of the sub-continent cook sweet rice for holy festivals, but recipes vary according to local influences. Some are lavish, others – like this recipe – simple, but still delicious. If you cannot find jaggery or palm sugar, substitute muscovado sugar.

300g basmati rice
125g jaggery* or palm sugar
50g ghee* or unsalted butter
4 tsp sugar
2 cloves
4 black peppercorns
2 green cardamom pods
5cm cassia bark or cinnamon stick
25g unsweetened desiccated coconut*, toasted
1 tsp fennel seeds

Wash the basmati rice in several changes of cold water, then leave to soak in cold water to cover for 15–20 minutes. Dissolve the jaggery or palm sugar in 125ml water; set aside.

Heat the ghee or butter in a heavy-based pan, add the 4 tsp sugar and cook to a golden caramel. Carefully add 600ml water, the whole spices, toasted coconut and fennel seeds, and bring to the boil.

Drain the rice and add to the pan. Cook on a medium heat for 10 minutes or until most of the water is absorbed, then stir in the jaggery water.

Cover the rice with a layer of foil or a damp muslin cloth and seal the pan with a tight-fitting lid. Either cook over a low heat on the hob, or in the oven at 180°C (160°C fan oven) mark 4, for 12–15 minutes. Uncover the rice, fork through and serve.

CHAPATTI

Basic Indian wholewheat bread   NORTH INDIA

Bread is sometimes referred to as the 'third hand' in India, especially in the north where it is a staple. Used as a utensil to scoop up sauce or dal, it also contrasts with, and enhances the food. Chapatti is known by various names, including *roti* and *phulka*. It is made with a special wholewheat flour, called *aatta* or chapatti flour – produced from wheat grown in the plains of Punjab, Uttar Pradesh and Bihar.

MAKES 10–12
250g aatta (chapatti flour)*, plus extra to dust
1 tsp salt
ghee* or butter, to serve (optional)

Sift the flour and salt together into a mixing bowl. Add 100ml water and mix well until smooth. Slowly knead in an extra 3–4 tbsp water until you have a soft dough. Cover with a damp cloth and rest for 15 minutes.

With floured hands, divide the dough into 10–12 equal pieces and shape into balls. Flatten each ball with the palm of your hand, then using your fingers, press it on a lightly floured surface and roll out to a 12cm disc.

Preheat a flat griddle. Lay a chapatti on the griddle and cook on a low heat for 1–2 minutes until bubbles appear on the surface. Turn and cook the other side for 1–2 minutes, or until both sides are speckled brown. Remove and keep warm, wrapped in a cloth, while you cook the rest.

Serve the hot chapattis smeared with a little ghee or butter if you like.

PARATHA

Flaky wholewheat bread NORTH INDIA

Parathas are made with chapatti dough, which is rolled out in the same way, then layered with ghee or butter and folded into various shapes. Punjabi parathas are usually round or triangular, whereas those in Uttar Pradesh are often square. In India, parathas are a breakfast item, savoured with a vegetable curry, or pickle and yogurt.

MAKES 5–6

250g aatta (chapatti flour)*

1 tsp salt

plain flour, to dust

3 tbsp ghee* or melted butter

Sift the flour and salt together into a mixing bowl. Add 100ml water and mix well until smooth. Slowly knead in an extra 3–4 tbsp water until you have a soft dough. Cover with a damp cloth and rest for 10 minutes.

Divide the dough into 5 or 6 portions and shape into balls. Flatten each ball with a rolling pin on a lightly floured surface and roll into 12cm discs.

Brush a thin layer of ghee or butter on top of each dough round and dust with a little flour, then fold the dough in half to enclose the butter. Apply another thin layer of ghee or butter and sprinkle lightly with flour, then fold in half once more to form a triangular shape. Press the dough firmly and roll out with a rolling pin, maintaining the triangular shape.

Preheat a flat griddle. Lay a paratha on the griddle and cook on a low heat for 1–2 minutes until bubbles appear on the surface. Turn and cook the other side for 1–2 minutes, or until both sides are speckled brown. Brush with butter and cook on each side for a further 30 seconds or until golden brown. Remove and keep warm while you cook the rest. Serve hot.

POORI

Deep-fried wholewheat bread NORTH INDIA

Pooris are made with the same dough as chapattis, but they are deep-fried into soft, light puffs, which can be eaten plain or stuffed with vegetables. They are typically eaten with a potato curry for breakfast in Indian homes. Pooris are also associated with religious functions and celebrations in India.

MAKES 20

250g aatta (chapatti flour)*

1 tsp salt

2 tbsp vegetable oil

vegetable oil, to deep-fry

Sift the flour and salt into a bowl and add the oil. Gradually mix in about 125ml water, to make a smooth, stiff dough. Knead the dough until smooth and pliable, then cover with a damp cloth and leave to rest for 30 minutes.

Knead the dough again and divide into 20 equal pieces. Roll each piece out into a 7.5cm disc. Heat the oil for deep-frying in a deep-fryer, wok or deep heavy-based pan to 180–190°C.

Deep-fry the poori, 2 or 3 at a time, for 1–2 minutes until they puff up. Turn and cook for a further 1 minute. Remove with a slotted spoon and drain on kitchen paper; keep warm while you cook the rest. Serve hot.

NAAN

Seeded leavened bread   NORTH INDIA

**This is the classic teardrop-shaped bread of the north, made from
white flour, leavened with yeast and traditionally cooked in a tandoor.**

Sprinkle the dried yeast and sugar into the warm milk in a bowl and set
aside for 20 minutes until frothy.

Sift the flour and salt together into a mixing bowl and add the yogurt,
yeast mixture and 2 tbsp of the butter. Knead well to make a smooth
dough and put into a lightly oiled bowl. Cover with a damp cloth and leave
to rise in a warm place for 3–4 hours until doubled in volume.

Divide the dough into 8 equal pieces, shape into balls and place on a
tray. Leave to prove in a warm place for 10 minutes. Preheat the oven to
220°C (200°C fan oven) mark 7.

To shape the naan, roll out each ball to a round, and then pull out one
side to form a teardrop shape. Brush the surface of each naan with butter
and sprinkle with the poppy and sesame seeds. Transfer to baking sheets
and bake in the hot oven, in batches, for 4–5 minutes until brown specks
appear on the surface.

Variation: Omit the poppy seeds. Brush the naan breads with butter and
sprinkle with the sesame seeds and 2–3 tbsp finely shredded blanched
almonds before baking.

MAKES 8

1 tbsp dried yeast

1 tsp sugar

150ml tepid milk

450g strong plain white (bread) flour

2 tsp salt

2 tbsp yogurt

3 tbsp melted butter, cooled

2 tbsp poppy seeds

1 tbsp sesame seeds

BHATURA

Deep-fried bread   PUNJAB, NORTH INDIA

**This bread is often paired with a chickpea curry – *channa masala*
(page 129) – and served as a simple meal. There are several versions
of bhatura – this is one of the easiest recipes.**

Sift the flour, salt and baking powder together into a bowl. Add the sugar,
egg, yogurt and 100ml water. Mix together and knead to a soft dough.
Knead the butter into the dough. Place in a lightly oiled bowl, cover with
a damp cloth and leave to rest for 2 hours to let the dough rise slightly.

Divide the dough into 12 equal portions and roll out on a lightly floured
surface into 10cm discs.

Heat the oil for deep-frying in a deep-fryer, wok or deep heavy-based
pan to 180–190°C. Deep-fry the bhatura, one or two at a time, for about
1–2 minutes until they puff up. Turn and cook on the other side for about
1 minute. Remove and drain on kitchen paper; keep warm while you cook
the rest. Serve hot.

MAKES 12

400g strong plain white (bread) flour, plus
     extra to dust

1 tsp salt

1 tsp baking powder

1 tsp sugar

1 egg

60g yogurt

1 tbsp melted butter

vegetable oil, to deep-fry

GAJJAR KI CHUTNEY

Carrot chutney NORTH INDIA

This chutney has been popular in my restaurant for some time. It goes well with salads and canapés.

Peel and grate the carrots, then spread out on a tray and leave to dry in the sun, in an airing cupboard, or above a warm stove for 30 minutes to draw out the moisture.

Put the ginger-garlic paste in a square of muslin, draw up the corners, twist together and squeeze tightly over a bowl to extract as much juice as possible; discard the residue.

Put the sugar and vinegar into a wok, kadhai or sauté pan over a low heat to dissolve the sugar, then bring to the boil. Add the carrots, ginger-garlic juice, spices and salt. Bring to a simmer and cook gently for about 1–1½ hours, stirring frequently, until the liquid has almost all evaporated. Add the raisins and simmer, stirring, for a further 5 minutes until the carrots are absolutely dry. Take off the heat and leave to cool.

Transfer the chutney to a sterilised jar, cover with a lid and leave to mature for at least 2 days before use. Store in a cool place for up to 4 weeks. Refrigerate after opening and eat within a week.

MAKES 1kg

1kg carrots
20g ginger-garlic paste*
300g sugar
250ml white vinegar
1 tsp coriander seeds
2 star anise
1½ tbsp red chilli powder
1 tbsp ground cumin
1 tbsp garam masala
1 tbsp salt
200g raisins

VENGAYA THUVAIYAL

Onion chutney SOUTH INDIA

This fresh onion chutney makes an excellent accompaniment to appetisers such as *momos* (Indian dim sum, page 16) and *karjikai* (coorgi vegetable puffs, page 19). In south India it is generally served with rice pancakes and steamed rice cakes, or simply eaten with steamed rice.

Soak the tamarind pulp in 4 tbsp warm water for 20 minutes, then strain through a fine sieve.

Heat 1 tbsp oil in a sauté pan and sauté the dried red chilli, green chillies, mustard seeds, black gram and asafoetida for 1–2 minutes until the mixture crackles. Remove and set aside.

Add the remaining oil to the pan and sauté the red onions until softened and lightly browned. Transfer the onions and spice mixture to a blender or mini-processor, add the coriander leaves, salt and tamarind liquid and whiz to a coarse paste. Transfer to a serving dish and eat the same day.

MAKES 200g

1 tbsp tamarind pulp*
3 tbsp vegetable oil
1 dried red chilli
2 green chillies, chopped
1½ tsp mustard seeds
3 tsp black gram*
¼ tsp asafoetida*
3 medium red onions, chopped
5 tbsp chopped coriander leaves
1 tsp salt

DHANIYA AUR MUNGFALI KI CHUTNEY

Coriander chutney NORTH AND WEST INDIA

This versatile, tangy chutney goes well with most Indian snacks and street foods. It also complements many fish and chicken dishes. For a milder flavour, reduce the number of chillies.

Put all the ingredients into a blender or mini-processor and whiz to a smooth paste. If the chutney is too thick, stir in a little water. Transfer to a serving dish and eat the same day.

MAKES 100g

100g coriander leaves, roughly chopped

4 green chillies, stem removed

1 tbsp chopped root ginger

2 garlic cloves, crushed

3 tbsp lemon juice

1 tbsp roasted black gram* or toasted peanuts

1/2 tsp salt

TETULER MISHTI CHOTNI

Sweet tamarind chutney WEST BENGAL, EAST INDIA

The chutneys of east India are amazingly different from those in other parts of the country. Bengalis certainly know how to balance their ingredients to perfection. This is a good accompaniment to fried snacks like samosas, as well as salads and some main dishes. It is prepared for special occasions in east India.

Soak the tamarind pulp in 250ml hot water for 20 minutes, then strain through a fine sieve into a bowl; discard the residue.

Add the grated jaggery, chilli powder, toasted spices and salt to the tamarind extract. If the chutney is too thick, stir in a little water.

Cool before serving, garnished with chopped coriander leaves. Eat this chutney on the day it is made.

MAKES 400g

150g dried tamarind pulp*

150g grated jaggery* or palm sugar

1 tsp chilli powder

1 tsp coriander seeds, toasted

1 tsp aniseed, toasted

1 tsp cumin seeds, toasted

1 1/2 tsp salt

2 tbsp chopped coriander leaves

DAHI AUR SARSON KI CHUTNEY

Mustard and yogurt chutney SOUTH INDIA

I serve this light, simple chutney with a variety of appetisers. It is always popular.

Whisk the yogurt with the honey, salt, chopped ginger and mint in a bowl and set aside.

Heat the oil in a pan, add the mustard seeds and turmeric and sauté until the mustard seeds start to sizzle. Add this spice mixture to the yogurt and mix well. Taste and adjust the sharpness with lime juice if required. Refrigerate and use within a day.

MAKES 300g

300g natural set yogurt

1 tbsp thin honey

1 tsp salt

1 1/2 tsp finely chopped root ginger

1 tbsp finely chopped mint

2 tsp vegetable oil

1/2 tsp mustard seeds

1/4 tsp ground turmeric

1 tsp lime juice, or to taste (optional)

BHUNE TIMATER KI CHUTNEY

Grilled tomato chutney NORTH AND EAST INDIA

This fresh chutney is particularly good with *momos* (Indian dim sum, page 16), but it can be served with many other starters, and as a side dish with chicken, lamb or fish.

Preheat the grill to high. Slit the tomato skins to prevent them bursting and place on the grill rack with the unpeeled garlic cloves. Grill, turning occasionally, until charred all over. Remove and cool slightly.

Coarsely chop the tomatoes and place in a bowl. Peel and chop the chargrilled garlic and add to the bowl with the green chilli, ginger, oil, lemon juice, cumin, salt and sugar. Mix well, then add the chopped coriander. Refrigerate and use this fresh chutney within a day.

MAKES 250g

4 medium tomatoes

4 garlic cloves (unpeeled)

1 green chilli, finely chopped

1 tsp finely chopped root ginger

1 tbsp vegetable oil

2 tbsp lemon juice

1 tsp cumin seeds, toasted and crushed

1 tsp salt

½ tsp sugar

2 tbsp finely chopped coriander leaves

TAMOTOR CHOTNI

Tomato chutney EAST INDIA

This tangy chutney complements most Indian snacks and street food.

Heat the oil in a pan, add all the spices with the whole dried chillies and sauté for 1–2 minutes until they crackle. Add the sugar and vinegar and slowly bring to a simmer to dissolve the sugar.

Add the tomatoes and salt, and cook on a low heat for about 1 hour, stirring frequently, until the tomatoes break down to a thick chutney consistency. Check the seasoning, then take off the heat.

Spoon into sterilised jars, cool, then seal with lids and store in a cool place for up to 2 months. Once opened, store in the fridge and consume within 2 weeks.

MAKES 600g

4 tbsp vegetable oil

1 tsp onion seeds

1 tsp fennel seeds

1 tsp cumin seeds

1 tsp mustard seeds

2 dried red chillies

350g palm sugar* or brown sugar

300ml white vinegar

1kg ripe tomatoes

1½ tsp salt, or to taste

LAHSUNI CHUTNEY

Garlic chutney NORTH INDIA

In India, this spicy chutney is traditionally prepared on a grinding stone, but a blender will also do the job.

Put all the ingredients into a blender or mini-processor and whiz to make a smooth paste, adding a little water if required. Store in an airtight container in the fridge and use within 2–3 days.

MAKES 200g

200g peeled garlic cloves

4 tbsp red chilli powder

4 tbsp lemon juice

1 tsp salt

AAM KI CHUTNEY

Mango chutney NORTH INDIA

An excellent chutney to accompany many of the starters in this book.

Peel the mangoes, cut the flesh from the stone, then grate and set aside.

Heat the oil in a pan and sauté the panch phoran for 1–2 minutes until the spices crackle. Add the sugar and vinegar and slowly bring to a simmer to dissolve the sugar. Add the ginger, salt and grated mangoes, and cook on a low heat for 30–45 minutes until the mangoes are tender.

Transfer to a sterilised jar, cool, then seal and leave to mature in a cool place for 1 week. Thereafter keep in the fridge and use within 2 weeks.

MAKES 600g

1kg large, full-flavoured green mangoes

3 tbsp vegetable oil

2 tsp panch phoran*

200g raw cane sugar

200ml white vinegar

50g root ginger, chopped

2 tsp salt

AAM AUR KRISHNA KAMAL CHUTNEY

Mango and passion fruit chutney GOA, WEST INDIA

This is a quick chutney if the ingredients are to hand. My Goan friend, Alphonso Pereira, taught me how to make it. For a thin chutney, add an extra 50ml coconut milk.

Scoop the pulp from the passion fruit into a small sieve over a bowl and press with the back of a spoon to extract the juice; discard the residue.

Tip the passion fruit juice into a blender or mini-processor, add all the remaining ingredients and whiz to a fine paste. Transfer to a bowl, cover and refrigerate until required. Use within a day.

MAKES 150g

2 passion fruit, halved

1 garlic clove, crushed

1 green chilli, stem removed

grated zest and juice of 1 lime

50ml coconut milk*

1 tsp palm sugar* or raw cane sugar

½ tsp salt

100g raw green mango flesh, roughly chopped

2 tbsp chopped mint leaves

PUDHINAE KI CHUTNEY

Mint chutney NORTH INDIA

This fresh-tasting chutney complements many Indian snacks and starters. It is very quick and easy to prepare. If you have mango powder in your storecupboard, add 1 tsp to the chutney with the chaat masala to enhance the flavour.

Put the mint leaves, coriander leaves, lemon juice, green chilli, red onion and ginger in a blender or mini-processor and whiz to a smooth paste. Transfer to a bowl.

Stir in the yogurt, chaat masala, chilli powder and salt to taste. Cover and refrigerate until required. Use within a day.

MAKES 300g

200g mint leaves

100g coriander leaves

3 tbsp lemon juice

1 green chilli, stem removed

½ red onion, roughly chopped

1 tbsp roughly chopped root ginger

5 tbsp Greek yogurt

1 tbsp chaat masala*

½ tsp red chilli powder

½ tsp salt, or to taste

ANARASHER CHOTNI

Pineapple chutney WEST BENGAL, EAST INDIA

Make this easy chutney to serve with snacks, and as a side dish.

Peel, quarter and core the pineapple, then finely dice the flesh.

Heat the oil in a pan, and add the bay leaf, cloves and mustard seeds. Sauté for 1–2 minutes until the spices splutter, then add the pineapple and salt. Cover and cook on a low heat, without adding any liquid, for about 15 minutes until the pineapple turns soft.

Add the jaggery or sugar and 3 tbsp water, stir to dissolve and cook for about 30 minutes until you have a chutney consistency. Cool, then spoon into a sterilised jar and seal. Keep in the fridge and eat within a week.

MAKES 300g

1 medium pineapple

1 tbsp mustard oil or vegetable oil

1 bay leaf

5 cloves

1 tsp mustard seeds

1 tsp salt

300g jaggery* or palm sugar

CHOTE SANTRAE KI CHUTNEY

Kumquat chutney NORTH INDIA

I invented this chutney to accompany the crab salad on my menu. It also goes well with many fish dishes.

Put the sliced kumquats in a heavy-based pan with the palm sugar, vinegar, cumin and coriander seeds, dried chillies, melon seeds and salt. Bring to a simmer, stirring, and cook for about 45 minutes – 1 hour until you have a thick chutney consistency.

Allow to cool, then spoon into a sterilised jar and seal. Store in the fridge and use within 2 weeks.

MAKES 500g

500g kumquats, thinly sliced

150g palm sugar* or raw cane sugar

150ml white vinegar

2 tsp cumin seeds, toasted and crushed

1 tsp coriander seeds, toasted and crushed

3 dried red chillies

2 tsp melon seeds, toasted

2 tsp salt

SAEB KI CHUTNEY

Apple chutney NORTH INDIA

My father taught me how to make this chutney and it has been one of my favourites for a long time. It goes well with chicken and lamb.

Peel, quarter and core the apples, then whiz to a purée in a blender or food processor. Immediately transfer to a heavy-based pan and add the ginger, spices, salt, sugar and vinegar. Bring to a simmer and cook gently, stirring frequently, for about 45 minutes until the mixture thickens. Remove from the heat and allow to cool.

Spoon the chutney into a sterilised jar, seal and store in a cool place for up to 2 weeks. Once opened, refrigerate and use within a week.

MAKES 750g

1kg cooking apples

1 tbsp finely chopped root ginger

1 tbsp cumin seeds, toasted and crushed

1 tbsp red chilli powder

2 tsp salt

200g sugar

200ml white vinegar

DESSERTS

Indian desserts and sweets are more complex and intriguing than most of us imagine, yet sadly this is where many people choose to part with Indian food. I have always featured a varied selection of Indian desserts on my menus, giving them a modern twist to heighten their appeal. From Muslim north to Hindu south, Catholic west to Buddhist east, desserts are influenced by religious festivals, and reflect their extraordinary diversity across the sub-continent. I encourage you to sample the varied recipes in this chapter and explore the intricate array of sweet Indian flavours.

RAVA KESARI

Semolina pudding SOUTH INDIA

This humble pudding is very popular in the south, but you will come across it in different guises all over India.

Heat the oil in a sauté pan, wok or kadhai and fry the cashew nuts and raisins for 2–3 minutes until the nuts are coloured and the raisins plump up. Remove and drain on kitchen paper; set aside. Drain off the oil.

Heat the butter in the pan and fry the semolina for about 10–15 minutes until golden brown in colour, with a nutty aroma. Slowly add 300ml hot water, stirring constantly to avoid lumps forming. Add the sugar, cardamom powder and infused saffron. Cook gently over a low heat for 5–7 minutes to blend the flavours. Stir in the coconut, cashew nuts and raisins, then remove from the heat.

Spread the mixture evenly in a greased shallow tin to a 2–3cm depth and allow to cool, then chill for 1 hour or until set. Cut into triangles or diamond-shaped pieces. Serve cold, topped with a spoonful of shrikhand and plum slices.

2 tbsp vegetable oil

10 cashew nuts

2 tbsp raisins

80g unsalted butter

250g semolina

200g caster sugar

1/4 tsp green cardamom powder

pinch of saffron threads, infused in 2 tbsp milk

2 tbsp grated fresh coconut*, toasted

TO SERVE:

80g shrikhand (sweetened thick yogurt, page 148)

1 plum, cut into thin slices

BADAMI PHIRNI

Almond and rice pudding NORTH INDIA

The best *phirni* I have ever tasted was made by Julie Sahni, a friend and celebrated Indian food writer from New York. This recipe is inspired by her.

Put the blanched almonds into a bowl, pour on 150ml boiling water and leave to soak for 30–40 minutes.

Using a blender or mini-processor, whiz the almonds and water to a fine paste. Strain through a sieve lined with a double layer of muslin into a bowl – squeezing the paste in the cloth to extract as much almond flavour as possible. Mix the rice flour with the almond liquid until smooth and set aside.

Combine the milk, cream and sugar in a heavy-based pan and slowly bring to the boil. Reduce the heat to a simmer and slowly pour in the almond and rice mixture, whisking constantly to avoid lumps. Cook on a low heat for about 10–15 minutes until the mixture starts to thicken and coat the back of the spoon. Remove from the heat.

Allow to cool completely, then pass through a fine sieve into a clean bowl. Stir in the rose water, cover and chill for 2–3 hours.

To serve, spoon the mixture into chilled dessert cups. Halve the pomegranates and scoop out the fleshy seeds. Spoon on top of the desserts and sprinkle with chopped almonds and pistachios.

50g blanched almonds

50g rice flour

300ml whole milk

500ml single cream

150g caster sugar

2 tsp rose water

TO SERVE:

2 pomegranates

2 tbsp blanched almonds, chopped

2 tbsp pistachio nuts, chopped

SAEB KI KHEER

Kashmiri apple pudding NORTH INDIA

My trainee chef, Imran Munir, showed me how to prepare this Kashmiri apple pudding. It is wonderfully versatile and complements many other desserts, or it can be served on its own.

Peel, quarter and core the apples, then cut into wedges. Meanwhile, put the granulated sugar and 600ml water in a heavy-based pan and heat gently until the sugar is dissolved. Add the apples, with the cassia or cinnamon, and cook for about 10 minutes until just soft. Allow to cool.

Put the milk in another heavy pan, bring to the boil and simmer, stirring often, for about 1 hour until reduced to almost a quarter of the original volume. Add the caster sugar, infused saffron, cardamom powder and apples. Heat, stirring, to dissolve the sugar and mix well.

Take off the heat and stir in the rose water. Allow to cool, then chill. Serve the apple pudding chilled, topped with pistachios and mint sprigs.

1kg apples

200g granulated sugar

5cm cassia bark or cinnamon stick

1.5 litres whole milk

100g caster sugar

pinch of saffron threads, infused in 1 tbsp warm milk

¼ tsp green cardamom powder

1 tsp rose water

TO SERVE:

1 tbsp pistachio nuts, roughly shredded

mint sprigs, to decorate

KHAJOOR KA KHAJA

Date and orange pastries NORTH INDIA

I have seen these crisp pastries sold in vast quantities during Muslim religious festivals in India. The authentic *khaja* pastry is somewhere between filo and puff pastry. Here I have used filo and drizzled the date pastries with a citrus cardamom sauce. For a delectable dessert, serve with a spoonful of Kashmiri apple pudding (above).

Mince the dates in a blender or mini-processor, then transfer to a small pan. Add the cumin seeds, orange juice and 100g butter. Cook on a low heat for 15–20 minutes, stirring occasionally. Remove from the heat, stir in the almond paste and kumquat or orange zest, then set aside to cool.

Brush one sheet of filo pastry with butter, lay another sheet on top and brush again with butter. Put two spoonfuls of date filling along one side and roll up the pastry to enclose the filling; twist the ends like a toffee wrapper to seal. Place on a greased baking tray and brush with butter. Repeat to make another 3 pastries, then rest in the fridge for 20 minutes.

Preheat the oven to 190°C (170°C fan oven) mark 5. Bake the pastries for 10–12 minutes until crisp and golden brown. Cool on a wire rack.

To make the sauce, put the orange juice, lemon juice, sugar and cardamom pods in a heavy-based pan. Heat gently to dissolve the sugar, then boil to reduce to a thick syrup. Allow to cool.

To serve, dust each pastry with icing sugar, cut diagonally in two and arrange on a plate. Drizzle with the citrus cardamom sauce.

300g pitted dates

1 tsp toasted cumin seeds, crushed

120ml orange juice

150g butter, melted

50g almond paste

finely pared zest of 20 kumquats or 1 orange, blanched and finely shredded

8 sheets of filo pastry, each 20cm square

icing sugar, to dust

SAUCE:

juice of 4 oranges

juice of 2 lemons

180g sugar

15 cardamom pods, bruised

GAJJAR KA HALWA

Carrot halwa PUNJAB, NORTH INDIA

This irresistible dessert is always in demand in Punjabi homes during the winter months. The authentic version is made with pure ghee, though I prefer to use unsalted butter. It's pure sin food – that's why it is so delicious!

Peel and grate the carrots; set aside. Pour the milk into a large sauté pan or other wide pan, bring to the boil and simmer, stirring often, until reduced to almost 1 litre; this will take about an hour.

Add the grated carrots to the reduced milk and return to the boil. Reduce the heat and simmer, stirring frequently, for about 1 hour until all the milk has evaporated.

Add the sugar and simmer, stirring, to dissolve. Continue to cook, stirring, until the carrots are quite dry. Add the ghee or butter and sauté well for 20–25 minutes. Stir in the cardamom powder, toasted melon seeds and raisins, then remove from the heat.

To serve, spoon the halwa into lightly greased 6–7cm cutters on individual plates. Smooth the surface to shape neatly, then carefully lift off the cutters. Top each serving with a spoonful of basundi and a mint sprig. Scatter chopped pistachios around the halwa. Serve warm.

Basundi: Put 2 litres whole milk in a large sauté pan or other wide pan. Bring to the boil and simmer for about 1½ hours, stirring frequently, until reduced to one-third of the original volume. Add 150g sugar and simmer for 3–5 minutes until the sugar dissolves. Add ½ tsp green cardamom powder and ¼ tsp saffron threads. Serve chilled.

1kg carrots
2 litres whole milk
200g granulated sugar
100g ghee* or unsalted butter
1 tsp green cardamom powder
1 tbsp melon seeds, toasted
1 tbsp raisins, soaked in warm water for 10 minutes, then drained

TO SERVE:
basundi (see left)
4 mint sprigs
2 tbsp chopped pistachio nuts

SHRIKHAND

Saffron and cardamom yogurt WEST INDIA

This Indian yogurt can be served as an accompaniment to various other puddings or as a light dessert on its own. In Mumbai, it is relished with poori (deep-fried puffed bread, page 135).

Put the thick yogurt in the middle of a muslin cloth, draw up the corners and tie together, then suspend over a bowl in a cool place for 2–3 hours to drain off the excess liquid from the yogurt.

Tip the drained yogurt into a clean bowl, add the sugar, saffron and cardamom and whisk lightly to combine. Spoon the yogurt into small bowls and refrigerate for 1 hour before serving.

Top with almonds and pistachio slivers to serve.

1kg thick Greek yogurt
150g caster sugar
pinch of saffron threads, infused in 1 tbsp warm milk
1 tsp green cardamom powder

TO DECORATE:
slivered blanched almonds
slivered pistachio nuts

BHAPA DOI E GOOLER MISHTI

Baked yogurt with figs in syrup EAST INDIA

This is prepared in a similar way to a crème caramel, but without eggs. Indian desserts – including the famous kulfi ice cream – are commonly thickened with *rabari*, or reduced milk, rather than eggs. Here I have cheated slightly and used condensed milk. To balance the sweetness, figs – known as *gooler* or *anjeer* in India – are poached in a spiced lemon syrup to serve alongside. These figs will complement many other desserts, too.

Preheat the oven to 150°C (130°C fan oven) mark 2. Line four ramekins with paper muffin cases.

Whisk the condensed milk, yogurt and cardamom powder together in a bowl, then fold in the pistachios and raisins. Pour the mixture into the lined ramekins. Stand them in a roasting tin and pour enough warm water into the tin to come almost halfway up the sides of the moulds. Bake in the oven for 40–50 minutes until set.

Meanwhile, prepare the figs. Put the sugar, 300ml water, the lemon zest and juice, and the spices in a small heavy-based pan and place over a low heat until the sugar has dissolved, then bring to the boil. In the meantime, cut each fig vertically into four. Add the figs to the sugar syrup and simmer for 2 minutes, then immediately take the pan off the heat. Leave the figs to cool in the syrup.

On removing the baked puddings from the oven, take the ramekins out of the water-bath and set aside to cool.

To serve, unmould the puddings on to serving plates, arrange the figs on top and drizzle a little of the poaching syrup around the plates.

Variation: If figs are out of season, try serving the baked yogurts topped with a scoop of blackberry or raspberry sorbet.

200g sweetened condensed milk

200g natural set or Greek yogurt

pinch of green cardamom powder

1 tbsp pistachio nuts, cut into slivers

1 tbsp raisins, soaked in warm water for 10 minutes, then drained

FIGS IN SYRUP:

4 ripe figs

2 tbsp granulated sugar

finely pared zest of 1 lemon

1 tsp lemon juice

2 cloves

2.5cm cassia bark or cinnamon stick

1 star anise

KAJU KULFI

Rich cashew nut ice cream NORTH AND WEST INDIA

This ice cream originated in north India but it is also very popular in Goa and along the Konkani coast of west India, where kulfi vendors on bicycles are a common sight. Sometimes they sell it with a dipping sauce made with seasonal fruits. Here, I have used raspberries.

Pour the milk into a heavy-based pan, add the cardamom powder and bring to the boil, then lower the heat. Simmer, stirring frequently, until the milk has reduced to one-third of the original volume and has a granular consistency; this will take about 1½ hours.

Take off the heat and stir in the sugar and crushed nuts. Return the pan to a low heat and stir until the sugar has dissolved. Remove from the heat and set aside to cool. Add the kewra water or rose essence, mix well, then cover and chill thoroughly. (If you have an ice-cream maker, churn the mixture for 30–45 minutes at this stage to refine the texture.)

Fill individual conical moulds, about 175ml capacity, with the kulfi mixture and freeze for 4–5 hours until firm.

To make the sauce, purée the raspberries with the icing sugar in a blender, then strain through a fine sieve into a bowl. Chill until required.

To serve, unmould the kulfi and slice each one into four pieces. Arrange on chilled plates and drizzle the raspberry sauce around. Serve at once.

2 litres whole milk

½ tsp green cardamom powder

400g granulated sugar

50g cashew nuts, lightly toasted and crushed

4 drops kewra water (screwpine flower essence)* or rose essence

RASPBERRY SAUCE:

100g raspberries

30g icing sugar, or to taste

TANDOORI PHAL

Roasted fruits NORTH INDIA

In India, cooking fruits in a tandoor is a common technique. As a variation on this theme, I marinate the fruits in a spiced honey and yogurt mixture before roasting in the oven or grilling. The result is delicious, and makes an excellent accompaniment to kulfi.

Cut the apples into large wedges, discarding the cores. Cut the pineapple, star fruit, papaya and mango into slices. Cut the banana into 3 or 4 pieces.

Mix together the ingredients for the marinade in a shallow dish, add the fruits, turn to coat and leave to marinate for 30 minutes.

Preheat the oven to 200°C (180°C fan oven) mark 6, or preheat the grill to high. Put the fruits in a roasting tin, or skewer them on to kebab skewers if grilling. Cook in the oven or under the grill for 7–10 minutes until charred on the surface. Serve warm, with kulfi (above) if you like.

2 apples (1 red, 1 green)

¼ pineapple, peeled and cored

1 star fruit

½ papaya, peeled

½ mango, peeled

1 banana, peeled

MARINADE:

1 tsp toasted sesame seeds

¼ tsp black peppercorns, freshly crushed

¼ tsp green cardamom powder

1 bay leaf

1 tsp grated lime zest

1 tsp lime juice

2 tbsp thin honey

3 tbsp yogurt

MENUS

● FIRST COURSE ● SECOND COURSE ● THIRD COURSE

SIMPLE MENU TO SERVE 3–4

● **ALOO TIKKI** page 23
Pan-fried potato cakes
DAHI AUR SARSON KI CHUTNEY page 138
Mustard and yogurt chutney
● **MEEN MOLEE** page 40
Keralan coconut fish curry
KEERAI PORIYAL page 111
Stir-fried spinach
TADKA DAL page 128
Home-style lentils
ARROZ COM COCO page 133
Coconut rice
● **RAVA KESARI** page 144
Semolina pudding

SIMPLE MENU TO SERVE 3–4

● **FOFOS** page 27
Goan fish croquettes
VELLARIKKAI KOSUMALLI page 32
Cucumber salad
● **CHUTNEY NI MURGI** page 60
Chicken cooked in tangy herb paste
MUTTAKOS KARAT THOREN page 115
Stir-fried cabbage and carrot with coconut
PAPPU DOSAKAI page 127
Pumpkin with lentils
ELUMICHAMPAZHA SADAM page 133
Lemon rice
CHAPATTI page 134
● **BADAMI PHIRNI** page 144
Almond and rice pudding

SIMPLE MENU TO SERVE 4–5

● **PAPARIS RECHEADOS** page 15
Stuffed poppadoms
AAM AUR KRISHNA KAMAL CHUTNEY page 140
Mango and passion fruit chutney
● **ISMAILI MACHCHI CURRY** page 47
Khoja fish curry
MURG HARA MASALA page 72
Herb flavoured chicken
BEGUN PORA page 106
Roasted aubergine mash
CHINA BODAM DIYE LAL SAAG page 115
Red chard with coriander and peanuts
BANGALI PULAO page 132
East Indian pulao
PARATHA page 135
● **KHAJOOR KA KHAJA** page 147
Date and orange pastries

MENU TO SERVE 4–5

● **MOMOS** page 16
Indian dim sum
LUQMI page 19
Spicy lamb pastries
TETULER MISHTI CHOTNI page 138
Sweet tamarind chutney
BHUNE TIMATER KI CHUTNEY page 139
Grilled tomato chutney
● **HARI MACHCHI** page 40
John Dory fried in green spice paste
CHAAP KARI VARUVAL page 89
Lamb chop curry
DHANIYAE AUR PYAZ KI KHUMBI page 121
Mushrooms with coriander leaves
ALOO DUM page 125
Potatoes cooked with melon seeds
TADKA DAL page 128
Home-style lentils
BANGALI PULAO page 132
East Indian pulao
CHAPATTI page 134
● **SAEB KI KHEER** page 147
Kashmiri apple pudding

MENU TO SERVE 4–6

● **JHINGA TIL TINKA** page 36
Deep-fried prawns with vermicelli coating
SALADE DE CARANGUEJOS page 36
Crab salad with coconut and curry leaves
● **TENGA** page 44
Sweet and sour fish curry
KOZHI VELLAI KAZHAMBU page 67
Tamilian white chicken curry
SAAG PANEER page 111
Spinach with fried paneer
ALOO PIAJ KOLI O TOMATOR TORKARI page 118
Spring onions with potatoes and tomatoes
TADKA DAL page 128
Home-style lentils
BANGALI PULAO page 132
East Indian pulao
NAAN page 136
● **SHRIKHAND** page 148
Saffron and cardamom yogurt

MENU TO SERVE 4–6

● **TANDOORI SUBJ CHAAT** page 32
Roasted vegetable salad

SHAMMI KEBAB page 24
Pan-fried lamb cakes

PUDHINAE KI CHUTNEY page 140
Mint chutney

● **NIMBUWALI MACHCHI** page 48
Tandoori salmon with lime marinade

ACHARI MURG page 71
Rajasthani pickled chicken curry

ALOO GOSHT SALAN page 94
Lamb with potatoes

DHAROSH CHACHHARI page 112
Spicy dry okra

PAPPU DOSAKAI page 127
Pumpkin with lentils

ELUMICHAMPAZHA SADAM page 133
Lemon rice

POORI page 135

● **BHAPA DOI E GOOLER MISHTI** page 151
Baked yogurt with figs in syrup

MENU TO SERVE 4–6

● **TANDOORI MURG** page 71
Tandoori spice roasted chicken

PUDHINAE KI CHUTNEY page 140
Mint chutney

SUNDAL page 35
Chickpea, mango and coconut salad

● **CHEMEEN MANGA CHARU** page 55
Prawn and green mango curry

NADIR GADH page 48
Fish curry with lotus stems

KAIRI KA GOSHT DO PIAZA page 90
Lamb in mango and onion sauce

KALLA VEETU KATHRIKKAI page 108
Chettiar aubergine curry

ALOO DUM page 125
Potatoes cooked with melon seeds

BANGALI PULAO page 132
East Indian pulao

PARATHA page 135

● **KHAJOOR KA KHAJA** page 147
Date and orange pastries

ELABORATE MENU TO SERVE 4–6

● **TANDOORI PANEER AUR HARI GOBI** page 31
Roasted paneer and broccoli

PUDHINAE KI CHUTNEY page 140
Mint chutney

● **CARIL DE CARANGUEJOS** page 56
Goan crab curry

HYDERBADI KALI MIRICH KA MURG page 64
Peppery chicken curry

VADAMA KARI KOZHAMBU page 85
Almond lamb curry

KEERAI PORIYAL page 111
Stir-fried spinach

SHALGAM MASALA page 122
Turnips with ginger and nigella seeds

KANDE KI SUBJI page 121
Spicy onions

BANGALI PULAO page 132
East Indian pulao

CHAPATTI page 134

● **KAJU KULFI** page 152
Rich cashew nut ice cream

TANDOORI PHAL page 152
Roasted fruits

ELABORATE MENU TO SERVE 5–7

● **RAJMA KE GELAWATI** page 23
Red kidney bean cakes

FOFOS page 27
Goan fish croquettes

TAMATOR CHOTNI page 139
Tomato chutney

● **MOCHHA CHINGRI MAACHHER MOLAI CURRY** page 55
Lobster curry with coconut

SURTI SANTARA NA CHHAL MA BATHAK page 77
Duck curry with orange

MARATHI NALLI GOSHT page 93
Marathi-style lamb shank

DAHAIWALE ALOO GOBI page 109
Cauliflower and potato curry

GANTH GOBI page 122
Kashmiri kholrabi

BANGALI PULAO page 132
East Indian pulao

PARATHA page 135

● **SAEB KI KHEER** page 147
Kashmiri apple pudding

KHAJOOR KA KHAJA page 147
Date and orange pastries

GLOSSARY

Aatta or chapatti flour
This is a type of wholewheat flour used in Indian homes to make unleavened Indian breads. It is made from Indian wheat that is low in gluten and soft-textured. This flour is ideal for flat breads because it has a low resistance to rolling. Although it is milled to a fine powder, Indian housewives still sieve it, to help aerate and clean the flour.

Asafoetida
This is a dried gum-like resin derived from *ferula* (giant fennel plants), which is also available ground as a powder. It lends an interesting flavour when used in small quantities, but in bulk it releases an overpowering smell. Asafoetida powder contains rice powder to prevent lumping. Of the various brands available, I prefer TRS. Use very sparingly.

Bengali garam masala
The term garam masala generally describes an aromatic blend of several dry roasted and ground warm spices. Every region in India has a few traditional recipes for garam masala. The composition of this Eastern spice blend varies, but the classic mixture is equal quantities of cloves, cinnamon and green cardamom with a couple of bay leaves, toasted and ground or blended to a fine powder. You can buy Bengali garam masala from most Asian food stores. Toasted garam masala is always added towards the end of the cooking unless otherwise stated.

Bengal gram
A type of lentil produced from black gram by removing its dark outer skin and splitting the kernel in two. Bengal gram is widely used all over India and features in main dishes as well as snack items. It is one of the main ingredients in western 'Bombay Mix'.

Black gram
Confusingly, this is a type of yellow pea, akin to chickpea, with its dark skin removed. It is used in various ways – as a lentil, snack or flavouring ingredient. Black gram can also be sprouted, or soaked overnight, then eaten raw in salads.

Chaat masala
A beige powdered spice blend with a tangy flavour, which is used as a salad seasoning in Indian cuisine. It is a combination of mango powder, black salt, asafoetida and powdered dried mint. Chaat masala is widely available from Asian food stores.

Coconut, fresh
Fresh coconut is an important ingredient in coastal India. To extract the flesh from a fresh coconut, push a skewer through the eye of the coconut and drain off the liquid, then crack open the nut. Remove the brown skin. The white flesh can be grated, finely sliced or shredded. Fresh coconut can also be deep-fried. You can also whiz roughly chopped coconut in a blender or mini-processor; this finely grates the flesh rather than reducing it to a paste. In this form, coconut freezes well with little loss of flavour.

Coconut, desiccated
Unsweetened desiccated coconut can be used as a substitute for fresh, but as it has a drier texture, I only use it in toasted form, as an alternative to freshly toasted coconut.

Coconut milk
This is prepared from fresh coconut flesh and should not be confused with the liquid inside a fresh coconut. To prepare coconut milk, soak 500g freshly grated coconut in 300ml tepid water for about 30 minutes, then whiz in a blender on high speed for several minutes. Strain the resultant purée though a fine-meshed sieve or muslin-lined strainer. You should have about 250ml. This first extract is called thick coconut milk, simply referred to as coconut milk in my recipes.

To make thin coconut milk, soak the residue (from the first extract) in another 300ml tepid water and repeat the process.

Canned coconut milk is available in cans and long-life packs. For use in my recipes, dilute it by 5–7% to obtain the right result.

Dried red Kashmiri chillies
Dried red chillies from Kashmir are big and broad. They are used either whole or crushed to a powder. These chillies are the best choice for making chilli paste to flavour marinades and enrich sauces.

Fenugreek leaf powder
Fenugreek seeds and leaves are two very different ingredients and not interchangeable. Dried fenugreek leaf powder is available from Asian food stores. Alternatively, you can dry fenugreek leaves on a tray in a cool warming oven, or other dry, warm place. Once dry, grind to a powder in a spice grinder, then pass through a sieve. Store in an airtight container to preserve the fragrance and flavour.

Fried onion paste
Made by puréeing deep-fried onions with yogurt, this paste is used as a base for sauces. To prepare, very finely slice 500g peeled onions, then deep-fry in hot oil until crisp and brown. Drain thoroughly on kitchen paper to remove excess oil, then blend with 50g yogurt to a fine paste. Store fried onion paste in a jar in the fridge, for up to 2 weeks.

Ghee
This clarified butter has long been the main cooking medium in north India, but with a growing awareness of healthy eating, oil is taking its place. I prefer to cook with vegetable oil and, if necessary, enrich the dish at the end with butter or perhaps ghee. If you want to use ghee, it is available in cans from supermarkets in this country.

Ginger paste
To prepare, peel and roughly chop 300g fresh root ginger and blend with 30ml cold water to make a fine paste, using a blender or mini-processor. Alternatively, grate the ginger using a fine grater, then mix with the water. Ginger paste can be frozen in an ice-cube tray for future use.

Ginger-garlic paste
This is widely used in my recipes. To prepare, blend equal quantities of peeled garlic and ginger with 10% of the total weight in water, using a blender or mini-processor. The paste should be smooth and very fine. Store in a sealed container in the fridge. If you wish to keep the ginger-garlic paste for longer, add 5% vegetable oil and 2% lemon juice as you blend the paste; this improves the keeping quality and lightens the colour of the paste. You can always freeze ginger-garlic paste in an ice-cube tray for future use.

Gram flour

Also called besan, this is a fine flour made from ground chickpeas. It is pale yellow in colour and has an excellent nutty flavour. Gram flour is used for breads, pancakes and coating batters for fritters, notably bhajis.

Green chilli paste

Green chillies range in heat from mild to devilishly hot. Most of their heat is stored within the seeds and white pith or *capillae* holding them inside the pod. Removing these seeds and white membrane takes away most of the heat. Green chilli paste is used where the flavour is required rather than the heat. To prepare, deseed green chillies and remove all white pith, then whiz to a paste in a blender or mini-processor with a little water and vegetable oil. Refrigerate and use within 3–5 days.

Jaggery and palm sugar

Jaggery is dark, raw sugar from the sugar cane plant. It has a distinctive taste and is less sweet than refined sugar. Palm sugar is made from the sap of various palm trees, such as date, coconut etc. Both sugars are loosely called *gur* in India. Used to enrich sauces and desserts, they are largely interchangeable in Indian cooking.

Kashmiri red chilli powder

Kashmiri chilli powder is used in Indian dishes more for its distinctive colour and flavour than for its heat. It has a strong flavouring impact on the food it is cooked with, especially when it is sautéed in oil, usually with other flavourings.

Kewra water (screwpine flower essence)

This is a scented flavouring obtained from the flower of the screwpine tree that grows mainly in southern India. Kewra is used in rice dishes, sweets and drinks.

Kokum

This is the dried skin of a fruit similar to mangosteen, which grows in coastal India. It is used to lend a sour flavour to curries and sauces during cooking but, as it can be overpowering, it is then removed from the dish and not eaten.

Mango powder and dried slices

Dried slices of unripe pale mango are used to lend a sour flavour and character to curries, chutneys and lentil dishes. Dried unripe mango is also available as a powder, known as *amchoor*. It is tangy and sour and used as a flavouring and souring agent in sauces and salad dressings. Both dried mango slices and mango powder are available from Asian food stores.

Mustard seed paste

Mustard paste is an unusual flavouring in Indian cooking and it is generally only used in the east. To prepare an authentic Indian mustard paste, whiz 200g black or brown mustard seeds with 2 tbsp water to a fine paste. Store in the fridge for up to a week or, to improve the keeping quality, mix with a little vegetable oil. A ready-made western-style mustard paste can be substituted.

Panch phoran

This unique spice mix is particular to Bengal in the north east. It comprises equal quantities of five strongly flavoured spices: onion seeds, fennel seeds, fenugreek seeds, cumin seeds and *radhuni* – a typical Bengali spice. If you can't get hold of *radhuni*, substitute mustard seeds.

Pomegranate seed powder

Sun-dried pomegranate seeds are used to impart a sour flavour to north Indian dishes. They are also available in powdered form from Asian food stores.

Saffron

This is the dried stigmas of the saffron crocus flower. As it takes many stigmas to produce a relatively small quantity of saffron it is an expensive spice, but only a little is required to impart a distinctive flavour and golden hue. I prefer to use saffron threads (also called strands) rather than powdered saffron, which is easily adulterated. To release the flavour, saffron threads need to be infused in warm water or other liquid. Pan-roasting saffron threads prior to infusing heightens the flavour. Infuse a pinch of saffron threads (or strands) in 2 tbsp tepid warm milk or water for about 30 minutes, then use as per recipe.

Sattu (roasted black gram flour)

In India, this flour is used as nutritious snack. Roasted black gram is ground to a fine flour, then sieved and kept in airtight containers. Mixed with chilled water, it is consumed to cool the body. Mixed with spices, it is used as a filling for breads and snacks.

Spices, grinding

This is an essential technique. Depending on the recipe, it may be dry grinding or wet grinding. In India, traditional stone grinders are giving way to mechanical blenders, though these don't develop the same depth of flavour. For dry grinding, use a spice grinder, mini-processor or pestle and mortar. For wet grinding, use a blender or mini-processor. Spices should be ground as specified in the recipe – to a coarse, fine or very fine paste or powder.

Spices, toasting

Toasting spices heightens their flavours. Use a heavy based frying pan or flat griddle and toast the spices over a medium-high heat, shaking the pan or stirring gently to avoid burning, until the spices pop and develop aroma. Once toasted, spices lose flavour quickly, so toast and use immediately. Sometimes, they are ground before being added to a dish, to bring out their flavour to the full. If possible, pound toasted spices using a pestle and mortar, rather than an electric grinder to retain maximum flavour.

Tamarind pulp

Tamarind is used as a tangy souring agent in Indian cooking. The flavour is derived from the pods of the tamarind tree. These are sold as seedless, dried compressed blocks, each 200g. This tamarind pulp needs to be macerated in hot water before use. Break up the pulp and soak in hot water for about 20 minutes to soften. Using your fingers, mix the pods with the water – the tamarind paste will become thicker. Strain through a sieve into a bowl, pressing to extract as much flavour as possible. The proportion of liquid to tamarind pulp varies according to the intensity of flavour required. For a thick paste, allow 400ml per 200g block. This can be stored in the fridge for 2–3 weeks, or frozen, then diluted before use.

INDEX